INDEPENDENT FEDERAL AGENCY COMPLIANCE WITH THE REGULATORY FLEXIBILITY ACT

GOVERNMENT PROCEDURES AND OPERATIONS

Additional books in this series can be found on Nova's website under the Series tab.

Additional E-books in this series can be found on Nova's website under the E-book tab.

BUSINESS ISSUES, COMPETITION AND ENTREPRENEURSHIP

Additional books in this series can be found on Nova's website under the Series tab.

Additional E-books in this series can be found on Nova's website under the E-book tab.

GOVERNMENT PROCEDURES AND OPERATIONS

INDEPENDENT FEDERAL AGENCY COMPLIANCE WITH THE REGULATORY FLEXIBILITY ACT

LANE JARVIS

AND

BILL LEIGHTON

EDITORS

nova publishers

New York

Library of Congress Cataloging-in-Publication Data

ISBN: 978-1-62948-195-1

Published by Nova Science Publishers, Inc. † *New York*

CONTENTS

PREFACE

As a group, independent federal agencies do less rigorous regulatory flexibility analysis than executive-branch agencies. The independent agencies rarely ever perform quantitative analysis of costs and impacts. Differences among the practices of most independent agencies that regulate small businesses, by comparison, were only differences of degree.

Chapter 1 - Independent federal agencies are subject to the Regulatory Flexibility Act, as amended (RFA). Because they fall outside of presidential authority, however, independent agencies are not subject either to executive orders concerning regulatory impact analysis or to OMB review of analysis. The absence of such guidance and oversight, characteristics of populations of entities regulated by independent agencies, and potentially differing adaptations or interpretations of regulatory flexibility raise questions about the degree and nature of their compliance with the RFA. Characterizing and assessing RFA compliance of independent federal agencies is the objective of this study.

As a group, independent federal agencies do less rigorous regulatory flexibility analysis than executive-branch agencies. The independent agencies rarely ever perform quantitative analysis of costs and impacts. Differences among the practices of most independent agencies that regulate small businesses, by comparison, were only differences of degree. The Federal Communications Commission (FCC) was a consistent exception.

Many independent federal agencies – one third of those in the study – do not regulate businesses or do not regulate at all. One agency had no final rules in the study period. Of the 13 independent agencies with final rules, six regulate financial institutions, two regulate aspects of safety, and five regulate other market activity.

Large businesses are much more prevalent in many industries regulated by independent agencies than in the economy as a whole. Five independent agencies regulate principally – or only – large businesses. Several other agencies reported individual regulations that do not affect industries containing, or activities practiced by, small entities.

A majority of rules by most independent agencies were exempt from the RFA or were certified as not having a significant impact on a substantial number of small businesses. The basis for certification (few small businesses and/or minor impacts) was generally plausible and clear, although the final rule notice sometimes did not have an actual certification. Agencies tended to be conservative about certifying: A basis for exemption was occasionally used as grounds for certification, and some rules that could have been certified were not.

Independent agencies generally had their own data, or could obtain data, on entities that they routinely regulated. Most of them consistently identified the type and number of small entities affected. The principal exceptions were regulations that went far beyond the populations routinely regulated, for which the numbers of small entities were clearly substantial. It usually was clear whether the number of affected small entities was substantial or not. The FCC, by contrast, used a mishmash of different size standards, industry definitions, and data sources, whose problems of incomparability, conflicting data, double-counting, imprecision, and lack of updating rendered the data unfit for analysis. The FCC repeatedly reused boilerplate industry descriptions that precluded any discussion of the specific regulation being considered.

Independent agencies generally provided a characterization of basic compliance activities, although the detail and precision was an area where the variation among the agencies was the greatest. The FCC's descriptions of compliance requirements were the most meager. Dollar costs were estimated in only a handful of cases.

Impacts usually were assessed qualitatively and (except for certification) more occasionally than systematically. Only one agency in one rule did a quantitative impact analysis complete enough to produce a cost estimate that was measured against a benchmark for "significant impacts." The FCC explicitly rejected the idea of impact analysis.

In many rulemakings, there reportedly were no comments on the Initial Regulatory Flexibility Analysis (IRFA). In response to comments that were reported, independent agencies generally provided a reasoned explanation for rejecting the suggestion or took some type of appropriate action to address an issue. The FCC repeatedly brushed off commenters' suggested alternatives without explanation.

Collectively, independent agencies used the full range of types of alternatives suggested in the RFA. Individually, almost every agency had at least one rule that incorporated a measure designed to minimize burdens. Some of the best crafted measures were developed by agencies that had only one or two rules in the study that affected small entities. Some measures were adopted to minimize burdens on small entities with specific characteristics that made them particularly vulnerable, rather than on the basis of size as such.

Some statutes were too specific to allow some regulatory flexibility alternatives, and financial regulators generally construed exemption as being inconsistent with their statutes. Yet for the most part, the independent agencies – except for the FCC – appeared ready to mitigate significant impacts that they were aware of. The sort of systematic search for and assessment of alternatives, which is based on quantitative analysis, however, was generally missing.

Chapter 2 - When government takes small businesses into consideration in developing regulations, it saves time and money for a vital sector of the nation's economy, our small businesses.

This primer on the Regulatory Flexibility Act (RFA) is designed to be used by those interested in the basics of federal regulatory compliance with respect to the RFA and Executive Order 13272. For more detailed guidance on the RFA, federal agency rule writers and policy analysts should refer to the Office of Advocacy's step-by-step manual: *A Guide for Government Agencies: How to Comply with the Regulatory Flexibility Act* (www.sba.gov/advo/laws/rfaguide.pdf).

The chief counsel for advocacy of the U.S. Small Business Administration has been designated to monitor agency compliance with the Regulatory Flexibility Act.

In: Independent Federal Agency Compliance ...   ISBN: 978-1-62948-195-1
Editors: L. Jarvis and B. Leighton   © 2013 Nova Science Publishers, Inc.

Chapter 1

INDEPENDENT REGULATORY AGENCY COMPLIANCE WITH THE REGULATORY FLEXIBILITY ACT[*]

Small Business Administration, Office of Advocacy

EXECUTIVE SUMMARY

Independent federal agencies are subject to the Regulatory Flexibility Act, as amended[1] (RFA). Because they fall outside of presidential authority, however, independent agencies are not subject either to executive orders concerning regulatory impact analysis or to OMB review of analysis. The absence of such guidance and oversight, characteristics of populations of entities regulated by independent agencies, and potentially differing adaptations or interpretations of regulatory flexibility raise questions about the degree and nature of their compliance with the RFA. Characterizing and assessing RFA compliance of independent federal agencies is the objective of this study.

As a group, independent federal agencies do less rigorous regulatory flexibility analysis than executive-branch agencies. The independent agencies rarely ever perform quantitative analysis of costs and impacts. Differences among the practices of most independent agencies that regulate small

---

[*] This report, released May 2013, was developed by Microeconomic Applications, Inc. under contract with the Small Business Administration, Office of Advocacy.

businesses, by comparison, were only differences of degree. The Federal Communications Commission (FCC) was a consistent exception.

Many independent federal agencies – one third of those in the study – do not regulate businesses[2] or do not regulate at all.[3] One agency[4] had no final rules in the study period.[5] Of the 13 independent agencies with final rules, six[6] regulate financial institutions, two[7] regulate aspects of safety, and five[8] regulate other market activity.

Large businesses are much more prevalent in many industries regulated by independent agencies than in the economy as a whole. Five independent agencies regulate principally[9] – or only[10] – large businesses. Several other agencies[11] reported individual regulations that do not affect industries containing, or activities practiced by, small entities.

A majority of rules by most independent agencies were exempt from the RFA or were certified as not having a significant impact on a substantial number of small businesses. The basis for certification (few small businesses and/or minor impacts) was generally plausible and clear, although the final rule notice sometimes did not have an actual certification. Agencies tended to be conservative about certifying: A basis for exemption was occasionally used as grounds for certification, and some rules that could have been certified were not.

Independent agencies generally had their own data, or could obtain data, on entities that they routinely regulated. Most of them consistently identified the type and number of small entities affected. The principal exceptions were regulations that went far beyond the populations routinely regulated, for which the numbers of small entities were clearly substantial. It usually was clear whether the number of affected small entities was substantial or not. The FCC, by contrast, used a mishmash of different size standards, industry definitions, and data sources, whose problems of incomparability, conflicting data, double-counting, imprecision, and lack of updating rendered the data unfit for analysis. The FCC repeatedly reused boilerplate industry descriptions that precluded any discussion of the specific regulation being considered.

Independent agencies generally provided a characterization of basic compliance activities, although the detail and precision was an area where the variation among the agencies was the greatest. The FCC's descriptions of compliance requirements were the most meager. Dollar costs were estimated in only a handful of cases.

Impacts usually were assessed qualitatively and (except for certification) more occasionally than systematically. Only one agency in one rule did a quantitative impact analysis complete enough to produce a cost estimate that was measured against a benchmark for "significant impacts." The FCC explicitly rejected the idea of impact analysis.

In many rulemakings, there reportedly were no comments on the Initial Regulatory Flexibility Analysis (IRFA). In response to comments that were reported, independent agencies generally provided a reasoned explanation for rejecting the suggestion or took some type of appropriate action to address an issue. The FCC repeatedly brushed off commenters' suggested alternatives without explanation.

Collectively, independent agencies used the full range of types of alternatives suggested in the RFA. Individually, almost every agency had at least one rule that incorporated a measure designed to minimize burdens. Some of the best crafted measures were developed by agencies that had only one or two rules in the study that affected small entities. Some measures were adopted to minimize burdens on small entities with specific characteristics that made them particularly vulnerable, rather than on the basis of size as such.

Some statutes were too specific to allow some regulatory flexibility alternatives, and financial regulators generally construed exemption as being inconsistent with their statutes. Yet for the most part, the independent agencies – except for the FCC – appeared ready to mitigate significant impacts that they were aware of. The sort of systematic search for and assessment of alternatives, which is based on quantitative analysis, however, was generally missing.

PART I

1. Introduction

A. *Background*

For 30 years, executive department agencies have conducted regulatory impact analyses subject to executive orders by President Reagan,[12] President Clinton,[13] President Bush,[14] and now President Obama.[15] Independent regulatory agencies (listed in Section C, below) are designated as such by statute. Because they fall outside of presidential authority, they are neither subject to executive orders concerning regulatory impact analysis, nor to OMB review.

The Regulatory Flexibility Act, as amended,[16] does apply to independent agencies,[17] although a few enumerated activities are excluded from the definition of "rule."[18] Thus, although not required to perform an E.O. 12866 regulatory impact analyses, independent agencies must comply with the Regulatory Flexibility Act. Among other requirements, this includes:

- Publication of a semi-annual regulatory agenda;[19]
- Publication of an initial regulatory flexibility analysis (IRFA) that describes:
  - "The impact of the proposed rule on small entities," which includes
    - "A description of and, where feasible, an estimate of the number of small entities to which the proposed rule will apply [and]
    - A description of the projected reporting, recordkeeping and other compliance requirements of the proposed rule, including an estimate of the classes of small entities which will be subject to the requirement and the type of professional skills necessary for preparation of the report or record;"[20] and
  - "Any significant alternatives to the proposed rule which accomplish the stated objectives of applicable statutes and which minimize any significant economic impact of the proposed rule on small entities;"[21] and
- Publication of a final regulatory flexibility analysis (IRFA), whose analysis parallels the IRFA, but which also must include:
  - "A summary of the significant issues raised by the public comments in response to the initial regulatory flexibility analysis, a summary of the assessment of the agency of such issues, and a statement of any changes made in the proposed rule as a result of such comments... and
  - A description of the steps the agency has taken to minimize the significant economic impact on small entities consistent with the stated objectives of applicable statutes, including a statement of the factual, policy, and legal reasons for selecting the alternative adopted in the final rule and why each one of the other significant alternatives to the rule considered by the agency which affect the impact on small entities was rejected."[22]

The reference to "significant economic impact" provides a checkpoint in the process. All rulemakings that fall under the public notice and comment requirements of the Administrative Procedures Act[23] must have an IRFA. If, during the IRFA, an agency develops a factual basis for certifying that the rule will not have a significant economic impact on a substantial number of small entities,[24] a FRFA is not required (although the APA still requires responses to comments).

B. The Study

Independent agencies are not subject to the analytical standards of OMB. They may regulate in substantially different economic environments. Financial regulation, for example, may play out differently than safety and health regulation. The mix of large and small entities may differ. Individual independent agencies also may have developed their own sense of what a regulatory impact analysis should look like, and the extent to which they refer to executive branch practice may vary. They also may have differing adaptations or interpretations of regulatory flexibility. These considerations raise questions about the degree and nature of compliance with the Regulatory Flexibility Act by independent agencies. Characterizing and assessing that compliance is the objective of this study.

The study was based on a review of final rules of the independent agencies over approximately an 18-month period. Regulations were reviewed if:

- They were listed in the Spring 2010, Fall 2010, or Spring 2011 Unified Agenda[25] as a "Final Rule Stage" or "Completed Action;" and
- The rulemaking actually had a final rule published.[26]

We reviewed each rulemaking, beginning with the RFA section in the latest Federal Register document. Where there was a finding of no significant impact on a substantial number of small entities, we reviewed the basis for that finding and the facts and reasoning that led to that conclusion. In such cases, a FRFA was not required, and the section in the preamble generally consisted of little more than that certification.

Where a FRFA had been completed, we reviewed the presentation of the regulatory flexibility analysis in the Final Rule notice, as well as provisions of the rule and other parts of the preamble. In some cases, we also used other sources, including the IRFA, additional comments, the listed agency contact, or an industry association. We wrote a brief summary of each rulemaking, formatted as seemed appropriate to the structure of the FRFA (which often followed the outline found in the RFA[27]). The individual agency case studies, found in Part II, were based on these summaries.

The purpose of the analysis was not so much to critique each regulatory impact analysis as to identify patterns that facilitate an understanding of the agency's approach to and practice of regulatory flexibility analysis. Part of these patterns reflected the mission of the agency and the nature of the regulated industry; part reflected the agency staff's understanding of regulatory flexibility. The analysis was judgmental to a considerable degree. The objective was to characterize distinctive aspects of the agency and of independent regulatory agencies as a group.

C. Independent Agencies

In some respects, understanding of regulatory practices is facilitated by grouping independent agencies by the type of entity or activity that they regulate.

Depository Financial Institutions

Independent federal agencies that regulate depository financial institutions include the following:

- **Farm Credit Administration (FCA).** The FCA provides credit and other services to agricultural producers, farmer-owned cooperatives, and other selected rural businesses.
- **Federal Deposit Insurance Corporation (FDIC).** The FDIC insures deposits in banks and thrift institutions, addressing risks to the deposit insurance funds, and intervenes to limit economic impacts when a bank or thrift institution fails.
- **Federal Reserve System (FRS).** The Board of Governors of the FRS supervises the financial services industry, regulates commercial banks and other depository institutions, oversees the nation's payments system, administers certain consumer protection regulations, and sets the nation's monetary policy.
- **National Credit Union Administration (NCUA).** The NCUA charters and regulates federal credit unions.

Non-Depository Financial Institutions

Independent federal agencies that regulate non-depository financial institutions include the following:

- **Commodity Futures Trading Commission (CFTC).** The CTFC regulates commodity futures and option markets to facilitate their competitive functioning, ensure their integrity, and protect market participants.

- **Securities and Exchange Commission (SEC).** The SEC enforces the federal securities laws and regulates the securities industry, the nation's stock and options exchanges, and other electronic securities markets, as well as participants in those markets.

Energy

Independent federal agencies that regulate businesses in the energy sector include the following:

- **Federal Energy Regulatory Commission (FERC).** The FERC regulates the interstate transmission of electricity, natural gas, and oil, as well as certain aspects of related infrastructure.
- **Nuclear Regulatory Commission (NRC).** The NRC regulates civilian use of nuclear materials – including reactors, nuclear waste, and other non-energy uses of nuclear materials - to protect the public health and safety.

Transportation

Independent federal agencies that regulate businesses in the transportation sector include the following:[28]

- **Federal Maritime Commission (FMC).** The FMC regulates ocean-borne transportation in the foreign commerce of the U.S.
- **Surface Transportation Board (STB).** The STB regulates railroad rates, service issues, and restructuring transactions of railroads and (to a limited extent) interstate trucking, ocean shipping, busses, and pipelines.[29]

Consumer Protection

Independent agencies that regulate commerce more broadly, especially with respect to consumer protection, include the following:

- **Consumer Product Safety Commission (CPSC).** The CPSC regulates consumer products, under authority from nearly a dozen statutes, to protect the public from unreasonable risks of injury or death.
- **Federal Trade Commission (FTC).** The FTC has a dual mandate that includes:
  - Anti-trust activities to promote and protect free competition, and

- Protection of consumers against unfair, deceptive, or fraudulent marketplace practices.

Federal Activity

Independent federal agencies that regulate quasi-federal organizations include the following:

- **Recovery Accountability and Transparency Board (RATB).** The RATB provides transparency and investigates fraud, waste, and mismanagement of American Recovery and Reinvestment Act funds.
- **Federal Housing Finance Agency (FHFA).** The FHFA regulates government-sponsored enterprises in the secondary mortgage markets:
  - The Federal Home Loan Mortgage Corporation (Fannie Mae),
  - The Federal National Mortgage Association (Freddie Mac), and
  - The 12 Federal Home Loan Banks.
- **Postal Regulatory Commission (PRC).** The PRC regulates the U. S. Postal Service.

Adjudicatory Agencies

Independent federal agencies that provide services of an administrative court include the following:

- **Federal Mine Safety and Health Review Commission (FMSHRC).** The FMSHRC provides administrative trial and appellate review of legal disputes arising under the Mine Act of 1977.
- **Occupational Safety and Health Review Commission (OSHRC).** The OSHRC provides administrative trial and appellate review under the Occupational Safety and Health Act of 1970.

Other Agencies

Independent federal agencies that have other distinct missions include the following:

- **Federal Communications Commission (FCC).** The FCC regulates interstate and international communications by radio, television, wire, satellite, and cable

- **Federal Election Commission (FEC).** The FEC administers and enforces the Federal Election Campaign Act, which governs the financing of federal elections.
- **National Indian Gaming Commission (NIGC).** The NIGC regulates gaming activities on Indian lands for the benefit of Indian tribes and to assure fair conduct of gaming.
- **National Labor Relations Board (NLRB).** The NLRB protects the rights of private sector employees to join together (with or without a union) to improve their wages and working conditions.

D. Overview of the Report

Findings of the study are presented below in two levels of detail.

- The next section (2) summarizes findings for independent agencies as a whole.
- Part II presents findings of case studies on each independent federal agency.

2. Observations and Summary of Findings

A. Entities Regulated by Independent Federal Agencies

Types of Regulation

The entities regulated by independent federal agencies have – as a group – characteristics that differ from entities regulated by many executive branch agencies.

- **Non-Business Activities.** Seven of the 21 independent federal agencies are not subject to the RFA because they do not regulate business activities.
  - Two agencies do not do any regulation as part of their activities because they were established to provide appellate review services.[30]
  - Three agencies regulate quasi-federal agencies and/or oversee federal programs.[31]
  - Two agencies regulate other activities that are not part of the private-sector economy.[32]

- **Financial Regulation.** Nine independent federal agencies, including half of the agencies with regulations reviewed in this study - regulate financial institutions and financial activities. These regulations tend to involve disclosure of information and business practices, rather than physical activities and tangible consequences.
  - Four agencies regulate depository financial institutions.[33]
  - Two agencies regulate non-depository financial institutions.[34]
  - Two agencies regulate aspects of consumer credit offered by depository financial institutions and non-financial institutions.[35]
  - Two agencies regulate other aspects of the financial system.[36]
- **Other Regulation.** Eight independent regulatory agencies regular other business activities.
  - Two agencies regulate safety.[37]
  - Six agencies regulate other market activity.[38]

Thirteen of these independent regulatory agencies published final rules during the study period.

Size of Regulated Entities

In contrast to the normal size distribution of industries, which is highly skewed with the vast majority of entities being small or very small, several independent federal agencies regulate only, or predominantly, large entities. Under these circumstances, the RFA does not apply to major classes of regulation.

- Two independent federal agencies did not regulate any small businesses.
  - The Farm Credit Administration (FCA) regulates the Farm Credit System (FCS). The FCS has a cooperative structure, under which all parts of the FCS are affiliated. Thus the FCS does not fit the definition of small entity.[39]
  - The Federal Maritime Commission (FMC) regulates oceanborne common carriers and marine terminal operators, all of which are large.
- Three independent federal agencies principally regulate industries that contain few, if any, small entities.
  - The Commodity Futures Trading Commission (CFTC) regulates several types of entities, which must register with the CFTC. Registration for most classes of entity has minimum asset

requirements. The CFTC defines "small" in terms of registration, so that the regulated entities in most classes of entity are large.[40]

- The Federal Energy Regulatory Commission (FERC) regulates interstate natural gas and oil pipelines and companies that provide interstate transmission of electricity. Fewer than 5 percent of these entities are small.[41]

- The Nuclear Regulatory Commission (NRC) regulates nuclear reactors and transport and disposal of nuclear waste, and all of these entities are large. A few NRC regulations concern other civilian use of nuclear materials, which involves a more conventional range of entity sizes.

- Some independent federal agencies regulate individual industry segments that contain no small entities. Examples of such industry segments found in this review include:
  - Direct broadcasting satellite providers, regulated by the FCC,
  - Class I railroads, regulated by the STB,
  - Corporate credit unions, regulated by the FCUA, and
  - Several types of entities regulated by the SEC.[42]

The relatively high prevalence of large regulated entities is a rather unusual regulatory environment. This is a major factor in certification that substantial numbers of small businesses are not affected. Among other implications, agencies that face this environment have relatively little experience in regulatory flexibility analysis.

B. Characteristics of Regulatory Flexibility Analysis

Performance of individual agencies was fairly consistent.[43] Differences between analyses of most independent agency analyses and analyses of major executive-branch regulatory agencies were substantially greater than differences among most of the independent agencies. The most obvious difference was that the independent agencies rarely, if ever, did quantitative impact analysis. Other differences derived from this one.

While there were differences in degree among performance of regulatory flexibility analysis by most of the independent agencies, the FCC was different in kind. Other agencies did a less-than-textbook regulatory flexibility analysis. The FCC essentially did none - while claiming to have fulfilled all the RFA requirements and denying that an impact analysis was required.[44]

Exemption and Certification

As a group, the independent federal agencies promulgated relatively few regulations that required a FRFA. Only thirteen of the 21 agencies had final rules published in the study period. Only three agencies[45] had more than ten – and only two other agencies[46] had more than two – regulations that were not either exempt from the RFA or certified as not having a significant impact on a substantial number of small entities. Agencies cited several bases for exemption:

- For a majority of agencies, at least one rule did not require the process of notice and public comment.[47]
- The Federal Reserve System (in adjusting reserve requirements)[48] and by the Federal Deposit Insurance Corporation (in resetting insurance premiums)[49] cited the RFA exemption for "a rule of particular applicability relating to rates."
- In one rule the CPSC cited an explicit exemption from the RFA in the enabling statute.[50]

Certification was based both on the lack of significant impacts[51] and on the insubstantial number of small businesses affected. Many agencies were somewhat inconsistent in their certification. In some rules it was missing, although it usually was possible to establish from other parts of the preamble that impacts were small. For the most part, the certifications appeared reasonable.[52] Where there was doubt, the agency generally did not attempt to certify.[53]

Need and Objectives

Most of the more substantive regulations were made in response to a relatively recent statutory change.[54] Some agencies have one basic authorizing statute, which was amended; others have many, with new legislation added to the list.[55] The Dodd-Frank Wall Street Reform and Consumer Protection Act (2010) drove regulations of almost all of the financial regulatory agencies during and after the time frame of this study.[56]

Statements of objective tended to start with the statutory objectives.[57] Quite often the objective was to implement certain provisions by "amendments" to the regulations. In many instances, the discussion tended toward a description of the provisions of the rule (which in some cases were dictated by the statute), rather than an explanation of them. The agencies generally provided a context for the regulatory flexibility analysis, but not much more.

A number of rules had simple, easily stated goals that were not driven by a statutory change. Examples include rules that made a clarification, defined something, updated a number, or resulted from a regular review. In such cases, the content of the rule was its own explanation.

Impacts on Small Businesses

Industry Profiles

In the rules reviewed, most of the independent agencies did a reasonably good job of identifying, describing, and estimating the numbers of entities that would be affected. Most of the agencies – particularly the financial regulation agencies - have data on the numbers and size characteristics of the entities that they routinely regulate, or else they could obtain needed data.[58] For most agencies – consumer credit being the most important general exception[59] – regulations applied fairly narrowly to an industry segment that the agency was familiar with. In almost all cases, however, the agency stopped with one class of "small," based on SBA – or its own[60] – size standards, so that the analysis usually did not consider very small entities as a separate class. The regulatory flexibility measures observed, however, did include thresholds and some exemptions of very small businesses with specific characteristics.

The FCC's license data, by contrast, lacked revenue information for size (except for wireline firms) and did not cover all the entities that the FCC regulated. Instead of developing or finding better data, the FCC used (sometimes for the same industry in one regulation) a mélange of several different types of data from several different sources[61] in combination with size standards from three different sources.[62] Problems of incomparability, conflicting data, double-counting, imprecision, and lack of updating, which the FCC did nothing to correct, rendered the data unfit for analysis.[63]

The FCC used six-digit NAICS industries and a set of industry groupings defined in terms of spectrum band or entity characteristics, which were almost completely unrelated to any specific regulation. Most analyses were far too broad, including far more industry groupings than could reasonably be explained. The FCC repeatedly reused boilerplate descriptions that precluded any discussion of the specific regulation being considered. As a result, the FCC failed to characterize clearly the actual scope of impacts.[64]

Compliance Requirements

Discussions of compliance requirements were (as the RFA states) "a description." This varied in depth from a list of compliance requirements[65] to a reasonably clear walk-though of the process of complying. If a form was involved, it was included in the notice; otherwise required information was described. Common topics included records to be kept, procedures to be developed, training, reprograming of operational systems, and (occasionally) modification of business models. For notices, alternative media and formats were often discussed. If multiple compliance alternatives were available – particularly when one alternative was a form – the options and their implications were generally spelled out. There were perceptible differences among agencies. Of those with more than half a dozen full FRFAs, the CPSC and the SEC were the most consistently detailed and thorough.

There were very few rules in which any dollar costs were estimated as part of a FRFA.[66] The agencies usually did not attempt even a rough estimate.[67] Indeed, in one rule the Federal Reserve responded to an SBA comment by pointing out that the RFA does not actually require dollar cost estimates.[68] Variation of compliance activities or costs with the size of entity was not generally considered, although the SEC was something of an exception.[69] Where small entities were considered separately, it was usually because a specific type of small entity faced distinctive issues under the rule.

Impact Analysis

A reasonably complete quantitative impact analysis was found in only one rulemaking - a joint rule that set registration requirements for depository institution employees who originate mortgages, as well as oversight requirements for their employers.[70] The rule involved *de minimis* requirements if employees originated fewer than five mortgages each. The agencies were able to estimate numbers of depository institutions that were subject to full requirements, subject to *de minimis* requirements, and not affected by the rule. Beyond that first step, only the FDIC had a complete analysis.[71]

Despite a lack of quantification, agencies did seem usually to have a rough understanding of the severity of burdens and an intuitive sense of what "significant" might mean.[72] In many cases, the impacts were rather clearly not significant. The analyses used ordinal comparisons: would some provision have less burden than another or how can a particular burden be reduced? On the whole, the agencies seemed willing to consider measures to reduce burdens on small entities when they saw the need of opportunity. In this respect, the agencies usually seemed reasonably responsive to comments. In general, however, the agencies did not visibly seek out such opportunities in a systematic manner.

The FCC, which lacked the data for impact analysis, denied that analysis of impacts was necessary – even for an industry that the rule (predictably) decimated.[73]

Response to Comments

Many of the rulemakings did not require a FRFA, and in a number of rules that had a FRFA no comments on the IRFA were reported.[74] For the most part, agencies appeared to provide considered responses to substantive comments included in the FRFA. Responses fell into several categories:

- The majority of suggestions were rejected – usually with an explanation.[75]
- The agency made changes in response to the comment, either by incorporating a suggestion or by otherwise addressing a concern. Most of the changes reported could be construed as some sort of regulatory flexibility alternative.
- Comments that compliance activities were understated evoked explanations,[76] but estimates were revised in at least one case.[77]
- In the joint rules, most agencies refined their quantitative analysis to some degree in response to SBA comments about the adequacy of the regulatory flexibility analysis.

Most comments evoked a discussion and explanations, but the critical comments on FCC rules routinely brought defiantly argumentative responses.

Steps Taken to Minimize Burdens

Collectively the agencies used a fairly wide range of regulatory flexibility alternatives, including effective use of all types of measures suggested in the RFA. There were, however, some constraints.

- Statuory mandates can be so specific that they eliminate most options for regulatory flexibility. Examples encountered include the following:
  - The Consumer Product Safety Improvement Act of 2008 required that CPSC safety standards be at least "substantially the same as such voluntary [industry] standards."[78]

- • The Financial Services Regulatory Relief Act of 2006 required agencies to develop a single joint model form to meet privacy notice requirements.[79]
- • The financial regulatory agencies declined to exempt small entities on the grounds that an exemption was incompatible with the law and/or the purposes of the regulation. The agencies expressed this as a matter of principle that occasionally rose to the level of equal protection under the laws.[80]

Differing Compliance Requirements
A number of rules included differing compliance requirements for small business, sometimes devised to address very specific problems.

- • **Partial Exceptions.** Some agencies designed specific exceptions or alternate provisions to address impacts on small businesses.
  - • The FTC provided a partial exemption to a ban on advanced fees that might have put small firms and sole practitioners owned by lawyers out of business.[81]
  - • An SEC rule that prohibited making payment to a third party for soliciting business from any government entity included a carefully crafted limited exception for small businesses, who are relatively likely to contract out marketing activities. In several disclosure rules the SEC retained previous limited exemptions for small businesses and/or added a new one.[82]
  - • The NCUA eliminated an exemption but grandfathered credit unions at current levels, but in a way that could only ratchet towards the underlying requirement.[83]
  - • Faced with a statutory mandate to create a single universal form, agencies included a menu of specific disclosures to allow customized descriptions of information collection policies of smaller businesses.
  - • An FCC rule concerning license auctions, provided small business auction bidding credits (a standard procedure) and auctioned small, partitionable service areas.[84]
- • **Alternative Compliance Procedures.** Some rules establish alternative methods for compliance, allowing the regulated entity to choose the less burdensome one.
  - • A joint FRS/FTC rule concerning risk-based pricing for credit offerings provided options for notification.[85]

- Some SEC rules provided voluntary alternatives to existing procedures.[86]
- **Timetables.** Some agencies extended compliance timetables to ease regulatory burdens in a variety of ways.
  - The CPSC extended the effective date of its crib safety regulation for two years to reduce the burden of replacing stocks of non-compliant cribs all at once.[87]
  - The SEC delayed compliance dates of two rules for small businesses by two years to allow small businesses to observe how the rule operates and prepare for implementation, and to give the SEC "a further opportunity to consider adjustments."[88]
  - The FRS and FTC also delayed the effective date of a joint rule.[89]
- **Tiering.** Tiered requirements were used in some rules so that smaller entities would bear relatively small burdens.
  - The NRC developed a three-tiered scheme, under which the annual assessment for very small entities was 8.5 percent of the assessment for large entities.[90]
  - A joint S.A.F.E. Mortgage Licensing Act rule included a *de minimis* provision that lowered costs for the smaller entities affected.[91]

Clarification, Consolidation, and/or Simplification of Requirements

Clarification was an ongoing issue. A number of regulations did little more than clarify a previous regulation and supply needed definitions. Clarification and simplification were often mentioned as objectives in developing forms, and in some cases considerable effort was devoted to this end.[92] Specific examples included:

- A FERC rule created an electronic version of a form that was clarified, streamlined, and accompanied by step-by-step instructions, and (the FERC believed) "should substantially reduce the burden of complying with EPAct 2005 cogeneration requirements."[93]
- In Regulation S-K, the SEC allowed small businesses to file an abbreviated report.[94]
- In a disclosure rule requiring a website "landing page," the FTC added the option of including the disclosure on every web page where the offer at issue was mentioned.[95]

Performance Standards

In the context of disclosure or reporting, a performance standard typically meant specifying the information needed without requiring a particular form or format. This approach was used most extensively by the FTC[96] and the SEC.[97] In another sense, CPSC standards were generally defined in terms of how products performed on tests, rather than how products were manufactured.[98]

Exemption

Exemption was not widely used. As noted above, the financial regulators declined on principal to exempt small businesses. The CPSC was constrained by statute from using exemptions, there were technological barriers for many FCC rules, and many other rules did not involve small businesses. Some types of exemption were found.

- Specific forms that were developed were often not mandatory. A joint statutorily mandated privacy notice form developed jointly by financial regulatory agencies was the prime example of a non-mandatory form, but there were others.[99]
- The two FERC rules that affected small businesses both had size thresholds.[100]
- The CPSC does not regulate businesses that are not registered, which coincides with the CPSC definition of "small."

Recap

Most of the independent agencies did reasonably well identifying the small businesses affected, characterizing compliance requirements, and certifying the lack of significant impact on substantial numbers of small businesses. Most of the agencies appeared willing to adopt regulatory flexibility alternatives - sometimes rather creatively – when the need or opportunity became apparent. Quantitative analysis of costs and impacts was almost entirely missing, however, as was the systematic search for and assessment of alternatives, which depends on such analysis.

The FCC, by contrast, did none of these steps with consistency or with enough precision to provide useful information; repeatedly brushed off both commenters' suggested alternatives and the idea of impact analysis; and exhibited a completely horizontal learning curve.

PART II: AGENCY CASE STUDIES

1. Commodity Futures Trading Commission

Overview
The Commodity Futures Trading Commission (CFTC)[101] is the independent agency responsible for regulating commodity futures and option markets. In 1974, when Congress created the CFTC, the majority of futures trading took place in the agricultural sector. Since then the futures industry has become increasingly varied over time and today encompasses a vast array of highly complex financial futures contracts. Objectives of CFTC regulation include:

- Fostering open, competitive, efficient, and financially sound markets;
- Protecting market participants against fraud, manipulation, abusive trading practices, and systemic risk related to derivatives;
- Ensuring the financial integrity of the clearing process; and
- Enabling the futures markets to serve the important function of providing a means for price discovery and offsetting price risk.

The CFTC requires an intermediary - any person or firm who acts on behalf of another person in connection with futures trading – to register. Intermediary registration categories that are the object of most CTFC regulations include:

- **Futures Commission Merchant (FCM):** An individual, association, partnership, corporation, or trust that solicits or accepts orders for the purchase or sale of any commodity for future delivery on or subject to the rules of any exchange and that accepts payment from or extends credit to those whose orders are accepted.
- **Commodity Pool Operators (CPO):** A person engaged in a business similar to an investment trust or a syndicate and who solicits or accepts funds, securities, or property for the purpose of trading commodity futures contracts or commodity options. The commodity pool operator either itself makes trading decisions on behalf of the pool or engages a commodity trading advisor to do so.
- **Commodity Trading Advisors (CTA):** A persons who, for pay, regularly engages in the business of advising others as to the value of commodity futures or options or the advisability of trading in

commodity futures or options, or issues analyses or reports concerning commodity futures or options.

- **Introducing Brokers (IB):** A person (other than a person registered as an associated person of a futures commission merchant) who is engaged in soliciting or in accepting orders for the purchase or sale of any commodity for future delivery on an exchange who does not accept any money, securities, or property to margin, guarantee, or secure any trades or contracts that result therefrom.

- **Derivatives Clearing Organization (DCO):** A clearing organization or similar entity that, in respect to a contract (1) enables each party to the contract to substitute, through novation or otherwise, the credit of the derivatives clearing organization for the credit of the parties; (2) arranges or provides, on a multilateral basis, for the settlement or netting of obligations resulting from such contracts; or (3) otherwise provides clearing services or arrangements that mutualize or transfer among participants in the derivatives clearing organization the credit risk arising from such contracts.

Regulation

The CFTC promulgated seven distinct[102] rules in the study period. These have included several types of rules:

- Two rules concerned relatively minor changes in reporting requirements for CPOs and FCMs;[103] and
- Two rules pertained principally to commodity brokers in bankruptcy;[104]
- One rule involved setting up a new framework to regulate off-exchange foreign exchange transactions and security-based swaps;[105]
- One interim rule mandated preservation of data pending final implementation of a comprehensive new regulatory framework for swaps and security-based swaps under the Dodd-Frank Act;[106]
- One rule provided a model privacy form,[107] which was adopted jointly with other agencies.[108]

Regulatory Flexibility Analysis

Definition of Small

When the Regulatory Flexibility Act was passed, the CFTC was faced with the issue of determining, for the purposes of the RFA, what was – or was not – a small entity. The CFTC developed its own size, based on two types of considerations:

- Setting its own definition was "premised on the limited usefulness, for Commission purposes, of the size standards for small business currently in use by the Small Business Administration." The SBA size standard for non-depository financial institutions is defined in terms of revenue. The CFTC considered a revenue standard, but concluded that it would be too unstable: "revenue tests would be subject to annual 'flip-flops' without any [change] in the number of customers."
- A central consideration of the CFTC was that "different regulatory treatment of registered FCMs would be contrary to the [Commodity Exchange] Act." Thus, it was not compatible with the CFTC's statutory mandate to have small and large entities under the same set of regulations that included regulatory flexibility alternatives.

To deal with these operational problems, the CFTC adopted a regulation that established a definition of "small entity," for purposes of the Regulatory Flexibility Act, that excluded any entity registered with the Commission from the definition of "small entity."[109]

This registration-based definition is operationally easy. It is less easily reduced to a simple number for entities that have a minimum net capital standard[110] that may be increased for an individual entity according to a variety of factors. FCMs, IBs, and OCOs must be registered with the CFTC to conduct business. The CFTC's view is that an entity that cannot meet the registration requirements has no business in the market. Thus there really is no such thing as a small FCM,[111] or small OCO;[112] CFTC regulations affect only large entities of these types.

CPOs also have a registration requirement, but they are exempt from registration if they are under a certain asset size (currently $400,000). The CPO exemption threshold provides a clear proxy size standard. It also acts as a sort of built-in regulatory flexibility alternative, because CFTC regulations do not affect unregistered CPOs. IBs have relatively low

CTAs do not fit the pattern. They have no assets and no convenient quantitative measure to distinguish between registered and unregistered. The CFTC declined to set a general quantitative size standard for CTAs, equivocating with language about rule-by-rule determination.

Simple Certification

In a majority of the rules reviewed, the CFTC certified that the rule would not have a significant impact on a substantial number of small entities.

- In three rules,[113] none of the affected entities was small by CFTC definition.
- One rule[114] affected CPOs and did not apply to small CPOs.

Good Cause Exemption

One rule[115] was an interim final rule, for which the CFTC found an exemption from the definition of "rule" used in the Regulatory Flexibility Act "when the agency for good cause finds that notice and public procedure thereon are impracticable, unnecessary, or contrary to the public interest." The CFTC stated:

> That good cause exists under 553(b) because delay in clarifying the scope of 2(h)(5)'s reporting and record preservation obligations will likely result in a substantial loss of material data relating to post-enactment pre-effective swaps that would assist the Commission in performing its oversight functions under the CEA.

The interim rule had little burden, because it merely required the preservation of existing data. A subsequent reporting rule, however, could well have significant impacts and would not be limited to entities that were "not small" by definition.

RFEDs

One rule[116] established a new category of registrant, the "retail foreign exchange dealer" (RFED). Entities within CFTC jurisdiction[117] that offer to be or act as counterparties to retail forex transactions were required to register with the CFTC as RFEDs. Congress set a stringent $20 million minimum net capital standard for registering as an RFED. Entities that engage in or intermediate retail foreign exchange transactions - principally "small" (unregistered) CTAs - were required to register with the CFTC under the appropriate category. The CFTC noted that "small" CTAs would incur relatively minor registration costs (an application, fee, and fingerprinting) but ignored substantial compliance costs of the rule itself, apparently on the grounds that the only entities affected are (after registering) not small.

Paradoxically, small CTAs morphed into large entities by registration, without any change in any size metric. Since these CTAs had to meet financial standards to register, however, they were not among the smallest of entities. In a broader sense, the CFTC was setting entry standards for the market, and if an entity could not meet them it was barred from entry. Technically, small entities were not affected (beyond transitional registration requirements), because:

- All FMCs and IBs are already large, by definition;
- Large CPOs are already large, and small CPOs cannot qualify anyway.[118]
- CTAs that can qualify really aren't very small anyway.

Model Privacy Form

One rule[119] involved the development of a form to provide initial and annual privacy notices to financial institution customers, as required by the privacy provisions in the Gramm-Leach-Bliley Act. The CFTC developed this form jointly with other financial regulatory agencies.[120] In this case, the CFTC identified CTAs and IBs "of all sizes" as being affected by the rule. This process of developing the form was extensive. Regulatory flexibility alternatives were constrained by the fact that the law required a single standardized form, so that information would be comparable across agencies. Agencies did regulatory flexibility analyses of varying depth. Some found significant impacts on a substantial number of entities that they regulated; others did not.

The CFTC appeared to have done one of the more cursory regulatory flexibility analyses. It is not possible to assess the contributions of any one agency to development of the form. The CFTC reached the following conclusion:

> Because use of the model privacy form is voluntary, and because its use is a form of substituted compliance with Part 160 and not a new mandatory burden, CFTC believes that the rule will not have a significant economic impact on a substantial number of small entities.

Cost-Benefit Analysis

The Commodity Exchange Act requires the CFTC to consider benefits and costs of any regulation it issues. This evaluation is required to be conducted under five broad areas of public concern:

- Protection of market participants and the public;
- Efficiency and competition;

- Financial integrity of futures markets and price discovery;
- Sound risk management practices; and
- Other public interest considerations.[121]

Assessment

The CFTC regulates certain financial markets and activities in those markets. In some instances, registration with the CFTC is a requirement to participate in those markets; in other instances not. In some respects, capital requirements for registration represent both the CFTC's view of the capacity the entities need and the threshold above which regulation is necessary.

The CFTC has opined that differential regulation of entities that are similar (except for size) would violate its statutory mandate. That is a principled policy position. The option of regulate or not regulate remains, however, and the CFTC does not appear to be concerned with regulation of the small end of the size spectrum. From that perspective, it makes a great deal of practical sense to make the regulated population coterminous with the entities that are "excluded" from being small.

The result is a threshold that functions in most cases like a standing regulatory flexibility partial exemption. Whatever its relationship to the SBA size standard (and that relationship is variable), it shields the smallest entities – those that a regulatory flexibility analysis should be most concerned with - from regulatory impacts. Because of the way it defines "small," the CFTC does not really do regulatory flexibility analysis in the conventional sense.

2. Consumer Product Safety Commission

Overview

The U.S. Consumer Product Safety Commission (CPSC)[122] is an independent Federal regulatory agency charged with protecting the public from unreasonable risks of injury or death from thousands of types of consumer products under the agency's jurisdiction. Such risks include fire, electrical, chemical, or mechanical hazards and injuries to children. The CPSC acts under authority of a number of federal laws, including:

- The Consumer Product Safety Act (CPSA);
- The Children's Gasoline Burn Prevention Act (CGCPA);
- The Child Safety Protection Act (CSPA);
- The Federal Hazardous Substances Act (FHSA);

- The Flammable Fabrics Act (FFA);
- The Poison Prevention Packaging Act (PPPA);
- The Refrigerator Safety Act (RSA);
- The Virginia Graeme Baker Pool and Spa Safety Act (P&SSA); and
- The Consumer Product Safety Improvement Act (CPSIA).

The CPSC uses a number of approaches to protect the public from safety risks, which include:

- Issuing and enforcing mandatory standards or banning consumer products if no feasible standard would adequately protect the public;
- Developing voluntary standards with industry;
- Obtaining the recall of products or arranging for their repair;
- Conducting research and testing on potential product hazards; and
- Informing and educating consumers through product labeling, the media, state and local governments, private organizations, and by responding to consumer inquiries.

Information is one of the CPSC's key tools. The CPSC National Injury Information Clearinghouse maintains and disseminates statistics and information relating to the prevention of death and injury associated with consumer products. Clearinghouse data are compiled from a variety of sources, including:

- The National Electronic Injury Surveillance System (NEISS), a sample of hospitals that are statistically representative of hospital emergency rooms nationwide;
- State Death Certificate Files;
- An In-Depth Investigations (INDP) File, which contains summaries of reports of investigations into events surrounding product-related injuries or incidents; and
- An Injury/Potential Injury Incident File (IPII), which contains summaries, indexed by consumer product, of Hotline reports, product related newspaper accounts, reports from medical examiners, and letters to CPSC.

The CPSC provides assistance to small business to make sure that products are in compliance with the applicable federal laws on consumer product safety. The Small Business Ombudsman serves as a dedicated resource for small businesses in CPSC-regulated industries, providing guidance and answering questions on technical issues related to CPSC's statutes, regulations, and regulatory processes.

Regulations

All of the CPSC rulemakings in the study period implemented aspects of the Consumer Product Safety Improvement Act of 2008 (CPSIA). The CPSIA was a sweeping law that covered a broad spectrum of products, of which children's products were particularly prominent in the resultant regulations. In some instances the CPSIA affected not only manufacturers but also downstream sellers and users of products.

The CPSC rules promulgated in the study period followed requirements of the CPSIA quite closely. These 19 rulemakings[123] included:

- Four rules that set mandatory standards for specific children's products,[124] which were voluntary industry standards with relatively minor additional provisions;
- Seven rules that established accreditation requirements for third-party conformity assessment bodies to test various products.[125]
- Three interpretive rules that expanded on provisions of terms used in the CPSIA, including:
- One rule that listed factors to be considered in determining civil penalties,[126] and
- Two rules that provided more precise definitions of statutory language;[127]
- Two minor technology-based changes in safety standards;[128] and
- Three standards related to information.[129]

Analysis

Regulatory Flexibility Analysis

Most of these rules can be grouped into classes for which the analysis was quite similar. The analysis tended to be somewhat free-form but addressed regulatory flexibility issues.

Standards for Children's Products

These standards were largely shaped by the CPSIA, which required the CPSC to:

Promulgate consumer safety standards that –

i.   are substantially the same as such voluntary standards; or
ii.   are more stringent than such voluntary standards if the Commission
       determines that more stringent standards would further reduce the risk
       of injury associated with such products.

In all cases the CPSC adopted the relevant ASTM standard and considered additional requirements. The additional provisions usually involved changes in the testing protocol. In the case of infant walkers, a new test was added, and this might require some product change.[130]

The CPSC described industries in terms of manufacturers and importers. Where downstream users were affected, the CPSC collected data on them as well. The CPSC obtained data on the numbers of entities of each type, as well as sufficient information to classify them by size (using SBA standards) in most cases. The CPSC also had certification data on compliance with the voluntary standards from the Juvenile Products Manufacturers Association.

The CPSC identified the types of costs that would be required for non-compliant products, but could not estimate them because the modifications required for any given out-ofcompliance manufacturer or importer were unknown and highly variable. Then CPSC pointed out, however, that importers were less likely to experience serious impacts than manufacturers, because they had more options – including getting their current suppliers to comply, changing suppliers, and discontinuing the non-compliant product and importing a substitute product instead. Where distinct sub-catgegories of a product were covered by the same rule (e.g., Full-Size Baby Cribs and Non-Full-Size Baby Cribs), each was analyzed separately.

The impact scenario was similar for all these products. Manufacturers and importers whose product already complied with the ASTM standard should incur minor impacts because the requirements that the CPSC added to the voluntary standards were incremental modifications. If products were not compliant with the ASTM standard,[131] however, costs might be substantial. If the affected product was a business's core product, impacts might be serious, and the CPSC acknowledged that some businesses might choose to leave the market place.

The crib standards raised distinctive issues, because the CPSIA coverage extended downstream from manufacturing. Two additional groups were affected:

- Retailers were required to certify their products. For new cribs, this would be straightforward, but sellers of used cribs might not be able to comply.
- Child care providers and public accommodations that supply cribs would have to comply. The CPSC estimated the cost of a new crib at $500. Options included using fewer cribs, using substitute products, and (for public accommodations) no longer supplying cribs. At between 4 and 45 cribs per facility, costs to child care providers could be substantial.

The CPSIA requirement that the standards essentially incorporate the voluntary industry standard limited regulatory flexibility options considerably. Exemption was not an option, and the scope for differential standards for small entities was quite limited. The CPSC considered promulgating just the ASTM standard, but concluded that there was little additional cost to the proposed standard. The serious impacts occurred when products did not meet the ASTM standard, and there was no flexibility there.

The rules did well by other regulatory flexibility standards. There were no reporting requirements and no recordkeeping requirements beyond certification of compliance. The standards were performance standards, in the sense that a test-worthy product could be designed and built in different ways (something the CPSC mentioned at times).

Cribs were a particular problem because of the potentially large stock of non-compliant cribs in use by child care providers and public accommodations and in the resale market. The CPSC noted the availability of substitutes and (particularly for public accommodations) the option of deploying fewer cribs, but did not consider that sufficient. To lessen the impacts, the CPSC extended the effective date for these rules by six months to allow retailers to sell inventories and extended it to two years for cribs used by child care facilities and public accommodations.

Accreditation Requirements for Third-party Conformity Assessment Bodies

The standard and the analysis in these seven rulemakings were almost identical. Section 102 of the CPSIA mandated that third party testing be conducted for certain children's products. In addition to independent conformity assessment bodies,[132] the CPSIA made provision for "firewalled" conformity assessment bodies[133] and "governmental participation."[134]

The CPSIA left specification of the basic accreditation requirements to the CPSC. The regulation required that all third party conformity assessment bodies must be accredited by an ILAC–MRA signatory accrediting body, and the accreditation must be registered with, and accepted by, the CPSC. The accreditation must be to ISO Standard ISO/IEC 17025:2005, "General Requirements for the Competence of Testing and Calibration Laboratories. The scope of the accreditation must expressly include testing to the test method for the specific product under ISO Standard ISO/IEC 17025:2005.

The CPSIA specified that testing by firewalled conformity assessment bodies be shielded from undue influence, that any attempt to "hide or exert due influence over the test result" be reported to the CPSC, and that confidentiality be assured. The CPSC added a rules to demonstrate probably compliance.[135] Requirements for government participation were set out in the CPSIA itself.[136]

None of these notices had a NPRM or went through the APA notice and comment process. Thus they were exempt from the RFA and were styled Notice of Requirements. The process would have given affected stakeholders an opportunity to comment on the proposed rules. Testing the safety of children's products (and thus accreditation) was voluntary, however, and requirements either followed existing voluntary industry standards or were mandated by law. Any impact would be difficult to assess and would probably be minor.

Interpretive Rules

The CPSC noted that interpretive rules are not subject to notice and comment and are thus exempt from the Regulatory Flexibility Act. The CPSIA had stipulsted the interpretative nature of the rules, and the minor procedural and definitional clarifications of these rules demonstrate the reason for this exemption.

Other Exemption

The CPSIA explicitly removed the RFA requirement for the rule on product registration for durable infant and toddler products.

Certification

The CPSC certified that the other rules would not have a significant impact on a substantial number of small businesses. The various factors cited in support of this conclusion included:

- The rule on lead in children's electronic devices provided a limited exemption, based on technical infeasibility, whose "only effect on businesses, including small businesses, will be to reduce the costs associated with compliance."

- The rule on mandatory recall notices:
  - Applies to a situation that occurs infrequently, and
  - Have content requirements that are largely dictated by the CPSIA.
- The bicycle regulation amendments:
  - Do not require additional testing or recordkeeping, and
  - Made minor rule changes that were not expected to require product modifications.
- The Consumer Product Safety Information Database rule:
  - Will rarely come into effect,
  - Would not disproportionately impact small businesses and might impact them less than proportionately,
  - Does not require a response (the action that would incur costs), and
  - Would involve only modest costs if a response is made.

In the case of the publicly available, searchable consumer product safety information database, a commenter pointed out that small businesses would require outside professionals to respond to a notice, argued that the CPSC had underestimated the cost, and suggested that the worst case scenario would apply to all affected small businesses. The CPSC responded by supplying calculations that it had done as part of the IRFA (which were consistent with the Paperwork Reduction Act analysis) and conceded that costs might be significant in a few cases but stated that this estimate would be the norm. The CPSC cited previous FOIA experience in support. The CPSC also noted that the new form of data was not the cause of incident reports that "would merit a large investigation effort," so that this cost should not be considered an impact. The CPSC showed that it had done its homework, both analytically and conceptually.

Assessment
The majority of CPSC rules were exempt from RFA requirements, and in most of the remaining rules the statute considerably constrained the available alternatives. The CPSC did an effective job of describing both the impacted industries and the nature and extent of the impacts, The certifications were credibly explained, as were the limitations on available alternatives. The CPSC did craft a reasonable measure – extending the effective date – where there

clearly was likely to be a significant impact on a substantial number of small entities.

3. Farm Credit Administration

Overview

The Farm Credit Administration (FCA) is an independent Federal agency, whose mission is to ensure a safe, sound, and dependable source of credit for agriculture and rural America. The Farm Credit System (FCS) - banks, associations, and related entities of the FCS, including the Federal Agricultural Mortgage Corporation (Farmer Mac) - is a nationwide network of lending institutions that are owned by their borrowers. This network has three levels:

- The Federal Farm Credit Banks Funding Corporation markets farm credit debt securities that the Credit Banks use to obtain a majority of their loan funds.
- Credit Banks[137] provide loan funds to Federal Credit System Associates. Credit Banks are prohibited by statute from taking deposits. These are large institutions, with assets running into the $10,000,000,000s.
- FCS Associates[138] act as agents of the Credit Banks, making retail short-, intermediate-, and long-term loans.

The FCS is the largest agricultural lender in the United States, and it provides credit and other services to agricultural producers, farmer-owned cooperatives, and other selected rural businesses.

The FCA Office of Regulatory Policy develops and issues regulations and guidance for FCS institutions to follow. The FCA Office of Examination examines FCS banks and associations to ensure their safety, soundness, and compliance with laws and regulations. If an FCS institution violates a law or regulation, or if its operations are unsafe or unsound, the FCA enforces corrective action. The FCA also protects the rights of borrowers, reports to Congress on the FCS financial condition and performance, and approves the issuance of FCS debt obligations.

Regulations

Ten "completed actions" were listed in the Unified Agenda in the study period. Of these regulations:

- One was a new rule – in response to requirements of a new statutory mandate;[139]
- Three involved relatively minor – or merely technical – changes to existing rules;[140]
- One announced approval of a voluntary joint and several liability reallocation agreement among Federal Credit System institutions;[141]
- One disposed of comments in response to a broad request for comments;[142] and
- Four noted completion of internal reviews, which resulted in no subsequent *Federal Register* notices.[143]

Analysis

Retrospective Review

The FCA does a considerable amount of retrospective regulatory review and has a well organized *Plan for Retrospective Analysis of Existing Rules*. This practice dates from long before Executive Orders 13579 and 13563 (from which FCA is exempt) – a fact that FCA is careful to note. As the *Plan* explains:

> Pursuant to the Farm Credit System Reform Act of 1996, FCA is statutorily required to continue its "comprehensive review of regulations governing the Farm Credit System to identify and eliminate, consistent with law, safety and soundness, all regulations that are unnecessary, unduly burdensome or costly, or not based on law." 12 U.S.C. § 2252. The FCA conducts this review every five years.

The number of published notices about reviews, rules scheduled in the *Regulatory Performance Plan*,[144] the responses to comments, and the efforts at simplification in the rules all tend to bear out this "regulatory philosophy."

While the *Plan* speaks of cost-benefit analysis, the notices reflect almost no quantitative analysis. The FCA refers to EO 12866. There is a fair amount of comparing alternatives to assess which is less burdensome and/or less necessary. Actual estimates of benefits or costs, however, are largely lacking.[145] The agency appears less concerned with net benefits than with specific policy goals. As the website puts it, "FCA develops policies and regulations that

- Implement the law;
- Promote the safety and soundness of FCS institutions; and

- Enable the FCS to meet its statutory mandate to lend to farmers, ranchers, their cooperatives, and other eligible borrowers in rural America."

Regulatory Flexibility Analysis

The FCA does not do regulatory flexibility analysis. No certification was given for the majority of these rules. On one rule, the FCA certified that there would not be a significant impact on a substantial number of small businesses on the basis that over 90 percent of small credit unions would qualify for a *de minimis* exception – but this rule was done jointly with other agencies and is not representative of FCA practice. In the three rules that involved only minor or technical changes, the FCA certified the rule with the following explanation:

> Each of the banks in the System, considered together with its affiliated associations, has assets and annual income in excess of the amounts that would qualify them as small entities. Therefore, System institutions are not "small entities" as defined in the Regulatory Flexibility Act.

The FCS is organized as a cooperative, which produces the inverse of the usual corporate ownership structure. FCS Associations own and control their funding banks, which (in turn) own the Funding Corporation. FCA Associations receive all of their funds from the Credit Banks. This is the sense in which FCA Associations are "affiliates" of large banks.

4. Federal Communications Commission

Overview

The Federal Communications Commission (FCC)[146] is an independent federal agency charged with regulating interstate and international communications by radio, television, wire, satellite and cable in the U.S. and its territories. The Communications Act of 1934 that established the FCC gave it the mission to:

> make available, so far as possible, to all people of the United States, without discrimination... rapid, efficient, Nation-wide and world-wide radio communications service with adequate facilities at reasonable charge.

To carry out this mission, the FCC has developed strategic goals in six areas:

- **Broadband.** All Americans should have affordable access to robust and reliable broadband products and services. Regulatory policies must promote technological neutrality, competition, investment, and innovation to ensure that broadband service providers have sufficient incentive to develop and offer such products and services.
- **Competition.** Competition in the provision of communications services, both domestically and overseas, supports the Nation's economy. The competitive framework for communications services should foster innovation and offer consumers reliable, meaningful choice in affordable services.
- **Spectrum.** Efficient and effective use of non-federal spectrum domestically and internationally promotes the growth and rapid deployment of innovative and efficient communications technologies and services.
- **Media.** The Nation's media regulations must promote competition, diversity and localism, and facilitate the transition to digital modes of delivery.
- **Public Safety and Homeland Security.** Communications during emergencies and crises must be available for public safety, health, defense, and emergency personnel, as well as consumers in need. The Nation's critical communications infrastructure must be reliable, interoperable, redundant, and rapidly restorable.
- **Modernize the FCC.** The FCC shall strive to be a highly productive, adaptive, and innovative organization that maximizes the benefit to stakeholders, staff, and management from effective systems, processes, resources, and organizations.[147]

FCC regulations, such as those reviewed in this study, generally are intended to implement these policies.

Regulations

Structure

The structure of FCC rulemakings is distinct from that of regulations by other agencies. For most agencies, the principal steps are a Notice of Proposed Rulemaking and a Final Rule – sometimes with an interim rule. Notices are organized in the Unified Agenda of Regulatory and Deregulatory Actions by RIN.

The FCC issues orders and organizes documents by docket. While FCC Unified Agenda listing have RINs, Federal Register notices generally have only docket numbers and FCC IDs. FCC orders come in different types, including Order, Report and Order, Memorandum Opinion and Order, Order on Reconsideration, and Order on Remand. Rulemakings do not so much propose and finalize a rule as start with principles or objectives and a request for comments and then evolve over time.[148] There may be several orders of each kind associated with a given RIN rulemaking – interspersed with numerous petitions for reconsideration and occasional court rulings. Important orders often are accompanied by approving and dissenting statements by individual commissioners. Orders are almost never really final; some contain a Further Notice of Proposed Rulemaking that raises further issues.

Dockets pertain to specific issues and may not be tied to any particular RIN. Frequently, one docket covers only part of the substance of what might be considered a rulemaking. The same order may appear in the histories of notices for several different Unified Agenda RINs. Orders pertaining to one docket usually also cover varying combinations of other dockets as well. It is rare that all dockets that might reasonably be considered part of one rulemaking are covered by one order, so that issues relating to impacts tend to be fragmented.[149]

This structure of sequences of orders with shifting content has implications for impact analysis. An impact analysis, and in particular a regulatory flexibility analysis, is specific to one order. Impacts of a series of orders pertaining to one docket become a moving target for analysis, and the baseline for impacts also shifts over time. Related impacts of related dockets become doubly complex. One rulemaking that was reviewed, for example, included eight Report and Orders over six years, involving a principal docket and three other dockets that were addressed in one or two of the orders. The evolving nature of rules, multiple orders for one docket, and kaleidoscopic combinations of dockets in one order may well be a significant disincentive to putting effort into impact or regulatory flexibility analysis.

Regulations Included in the Study
The study reviewed 16 FCC rules that were described as Completed Actions in the Spring 2010, Fall 2010, or Spring 2011 Unified Agenda listings.[150]

- Five new rules modified operating rules;[151]
- One rule principally reconfigured spectrum to free up spectrum for new use;[152]
- Three rules assigned spectrum to new service or allowed existing services to operate in additional spectrum;[153]
- Three rules concerned licensing or unlicensed operations;[154]
- Two rules concerned FCC procedures;[155]
- One rule required participation in a consumer education campaign on DTV;[156] and
- One rule required DBS licensees to provide capacity for noncommercial programming.[157]

In addition, to obtain more depth, the review included two rules outside the regular sample frame that were known to be of major significance:

- A recent rule concerning the open internet;[158] and
- An older rule, which was a major milestone in implementing Section 251 of the Telecommunications Act of 1996.[159]

Analysis

Regulatory Flexibility Analysis
When the FCC performed a regulatory flexibility analysis, it closely followed the outline provided in the RFA.

Certification
The FCC certified that two of the rules reviewed would not have a significant impact on a substantial number of small entities.

- One rule affected only large entities (direct broadcasting satellite providers).
- In one rule two brief explanations were provided:
  - There would be no interference with other users of the spectrum, and
  - Changes "will not affect any party legally manufacturing or marketing UWB devices."

In addition, no regulatory flexibility analysis was done for one rule because "the rule amendments... involve rules of agency organization, procedure, and practice."

Need for, and Objectives of, the Rules

Most of the FCC rules had a fairly specific purpose (other than simply implementing a statute), which was related to the FCC's strategic goals. Most also stated some type of operational objective to achieve that goal. The specifics varied:

- Four rules had goals of improving services to the public.[160]
- Six rules had goals of increasing operating efficiency and/or responding to new technology.[161]
- Two rules were the result of reviews, including: A routine periodic review of regulations, and The Triennial Review Order, which was a complex mixture of periodic review of regulations implementing Section 251 and response to court orders.
- One rule was designed to enhance the management, transparency, and fairness of a petition process.
- One rule was issued to educate consumers about digital television, thus facilitating the transition to digital television broadcasting.
- One rule stated very broad goals concerning enhancing the internet.[162]

In general, the FCC rules were reasonably clear in stating what they were trying to achieve and how. The Triennial Review Order and the Open Internet rule were exceptions.

Summary of Significant Issues Raised by the Public Comments in Response to the IRFA

In 12 of the 15 rulemakings in which a regulatory flexibility analysis was performed, the FCC stated that there had been no comments "specifically about the IRFA" or no comments at all. In three of these cases an issue was discussed in the FRFA;[163] in two others, the FCC stated that comments related to small businesses had been addressed (although where was not clear).

In three rules, there were comments about the IRFA that were discussed in the FRFA, including multiple comments both in the Triennial Review Order (and Order on Remand) and in the Open Internet rule. One commenter simply sought clarification of the rule, which the FCC supplied. Other reported comments were more critical, and the FCC consistently contested these.

Commenters in two rules raised concerns about the adequacy of notification of small entities that might be affected:

- In one rule, a commenter was concerned about the lack of reference to local exchange carriers (LECs) in the IRFA.
- In one rule, a commenter said that the FCC had "taken inadequate steps to notify small businesses" and failed "to conduct proper outreach to small businesses."

In both cases, the FCC's basic response was to say that it had given notice to the small entities in question and to cite comments from those entities as evidence. In the latter case, the FCC added that it had taken "several" of the steps suggested in § 609 of the RFA.[164] These steps were relatively passive, rather than being proactive outreach, and are not necessarily sufficient to "assure that small entities have been given an opportunity to participate in the rulemaking."[165] One step suggested in § 609 that the FCC did not say it had taken, for example, was "the direct notification of interested small entities."

Several commenters pointed to fundamental failures to follow basic procedural requirements of the law:

- Some comments, in essence, suggested that the FCC had not complied with the Regulatory Flexibility Act.[166] The FCC responded that it had "fully" satisfied its obligations under the RFA in this FRFA and pointed to some particulars that it clearly had done (e.g., give the SBA Office of Advocacy advanced notice). The extent to which the FCC actually satisfied its obligations is the subject of this research. To say that the FCC "fully" satisfied its RFA obligations – elsewhere the word "precisely" was used – really dismisses the comment rather than responds to it.
- SBA Advocacy commented that "the manner in which the FCC presented the issues in the Triennial Review is more consistent with a Notice of Inquiry ("NOI") than an NPRM" and that this did not allow small businesses the opportunity to comment meaningfully on the rule.[167]

This latter comment goes to the heart of the FCC's conformity to the notice-and-comment process. SBA advocacy explained:

The Commission's NPRM did not propose the actual terms or drafts of regulatory text and the FCC did not single out particular network elements to be removed from the unbundled network checklist... Unless the agency issues another rulemaking detailing specific rules, the Commission would be adopting rules on which the public would not have had a chance to comment. This lack of specificity is not consistent with the Administrative Procedure Act and frustrates the spirit of the RFA [which] anticipates that a proposed rule provides notice to small businesses of the regulations the federal agency is considering adopting.

The FCC's response did not so much address the comment as confirm it:

The Commission expressly sought comment "on applying the unbundling analysis to define the network elements" subject to unbundling, and indicated its intention to "probe whether and to what extent we should adopt a more sophisticated, refined unbundling analysis." The Commission also specifically stated its intention to reexamine unbundling obligations with respect to loops, switching, interoffice transport, OSS, call-related signaling, and call-related databases. We are thus not persuaded that the Notice somehow failed to signal the Commission's intent to examine rules that might result in modification of the list of elements (including possible removal of elements) subject to section 251(c)(3)'s unbundling requirements.

SBA Advocacy's point was correct; the NPRM contained no proposed rule, and it did read like an NOI.[168] The FCC promulgated the rule without giving the public, including small business, an opportunity to comment on this rule. In the case of this rule (the Triennial Review Order), this failure to allow comment was particularly striking. Two months after the NPRM was published the FCC argued a case concerning the regulations to be amended before the U.S. Court of Appeals.[169] The Court ruled against the FCC in many respects. The resulting final rule followed the Court's direction and reversed direction on some issues that the Court had remanded for further consideration. The Triennial Review Order represented a very substantial change in direction from the FCC's own thinking at the time of the NPRM. These events considerably compounded the FCC's initial failure to provide an adequate basis for comment.

Some comments on the Triennial Review Order IRFA pointed to flaws in the FCC's estimates of the number of small entities affected:

- One issue was the use of "boilerplate" language that differs little (if at all) in IRFAs prepared for various proceedings. The FCC responded that the commenter "has suggested no reason why the use of similar language in several proceedings is at all problematic" and added that similar language was justifiable for "a class that is likely to differ little, if at all, among industry-wide rulemakings such as this." The FCC might have had a point if the "similar" language was used for concurrent, closely related proceedings. The real issue was that the same language was used for all sorts of proceedings over many years. "Boilerplate" is an accurate description of the rather eerie repetition. This issue is discussed further below, but the central problem is that boilerplate precludes any regulation-specific content.

- The other issue was the use of seven-year-old Economic Census data that failed to capture rapid recent growth of an important industry (ISPs). The FCC responded that it had used "the most recent Census Bureau data." The FCC was correct in a narrow sense. The Economic Census is a quinquennial study, it takes three or four years for the data to become available, so that available data may be eight or nine years old. The timing of this rulemaking was unfortunate. The real issue, however, was the FCC's lack of initiative in finding more current appropriate data.[170] There is no excuse in relying solely on seven-year old data just because "the Census Bureau is... a source on which we have consistently relied." The Census Bureau's annual *County Business Patterns*[171] is available with about an 18 month lag, so that 2002 Census data *were* available for the analysis in question. In addition, the commenter proffered industry data. The FCC response showed no concern about using current data, stating that updating to 1997 data "would not, we believe, have affected a small entity's decisions concerning IRFA."

The use of boilerplate was universal in the analyses reviewed. The FCC usually updated data, but not always consistently or in an entirely timely manner. These issues are discussed further below.

One rule included a specific request for a regulatory alternative. A very small ILEC stated that it would like the Commission to use the data that it regularly receives from carriers to set a carrier size where exemptions from proposed rules and less complex reporting requirements can be set.

The FCC responded that an exemption was unnecessary for this rule because the costs were small, adding:

> We note that [the ILEC] does not cite any particular source of increased costs, or attempt to estimate costs of compliance.

The FCC's handling of small business issues generally was elusive. In the responses to comments in the Triennial Review Order, the FCC took a defensive posture.

> As an initial matter, we reject the contention that the Commission failed to consider the needs of small business customers of competitive LECs in fashioning the analysis set forth in this Order. We have grappled, throughout this proceeding and throughout this Order, with consequences our determinations will have on all market participants, including those on small business providers and small business end users about which [the commenters] express concern. We have also considered various alternatives to the rules we adopt, and have stated the reasons for rejecting these alternative rules, as commenters have urged. A summary of our analysis regarding small business concerns, and of alternative rules that we considered in light of those concerns, is presented in subsection 5 of the FRFA [steps taken to minimize impacts].

The text of subsection 5 contained a single sentence:

> Finally, we considered and rejected a number of suggested approaches to impairment.[172]

A comment that the IRFA "did not consider the impact of delisting unbundled network elements... on small competitive local exchange carriers" met a similar response: "We note that we have considered the concerns of competitive LECs throughout this Order, and those considerations are summarized in Part X.A.5, below." Part X.A.5 did discuss some issues,[173] but this was not an impact analysis. At best, an analysis was vaguely indicated, but neither described nor summarized:

> Through our granular impairment analysis, we have considered the resources and needs of various carriers, including small businesses, and have examined the state of the marketplace to determine whether it was economically feasible for competitors to self-provision network elements or obtain them from competitive sources other than incumbent LECs.

One commenter noted that the RFA requires an impact study on how an agency's regulations will harm small businesses,[174] and pointed out that the

FCC had not done anything of the sort for this proceeding. The FCC responded:

> We disagree: the RFA requires us to provide precisely the information contained in this FRFA, but does not mandate a separate "impact study." The Commission has therefore satisfied its RFA obligations.

In the Triennial Review Order, the impact on ISPs was a major concern of some commenters. The FCC responded by denying any obligation to consider these impacts:

> The RFA only requires the Commission to consider the impact on entities directly subject to our rules. The RFA is not applicable to ISPs because, as we previously noted, ISPs are only indirectly affected by our unbundling actions. In the interest of ensuring notice to all interested parties and out of an abundance of caution, we have previously included ISPs among the entities potentially indirectly affected by our unbundling rules, although we have been explicit in emphasizing that ISPs are only indirectly affected by these rules. On this subject, we note that the D.C. Circuit "has consistently held that the RFA imposes no obligation to conduct a small entity impact analysis of effects on entities which [the agency conducting the analysis] does not regulate." Thus, we emphasize that the RFA imposes no independent obligation to examine the effects an agency's action will have on the customers, clients, or end users of the companies it regulates – including ISPs – unless such entities are, themselves, subject to regulation by the agency.

The FCC cited several court cases,[175] whose applicability depends on the definition of "indirect." These cases developed two clear and distinct meanings for "indirect" effects of regulation:

- "Indirect" refers to a federal agency regulating through a state regulatory agency because:
  - The federal agency has delegated authority to the state agency (either directly or through a waiver), so that the federal authority sets the parameters of the regulation, while the state authority is responsible for the sort of details that would affect the distribution of impacts, or

- The state regulatory agency has the primary authority, so that the federal agency would be encroaching on state authority if it regulated directly.
- "Indirect" refers to impacts on customers in the form of passing costs of the regulated entities through to (state-regulated) customers as higher prices.[176]

The FCC's argument appears to have been correct with respect to impacts on the general public.[177] The facts with respect to ISPs, however, are quite distinct. The FCC was not regulating indirectly through a state regulatory agency; it has direct authority over ISPs. ISPs were more than just customers; they were competitors. ISPs were affected primarily through the terms of unbundling that were a set in the regulation, not by price changes resulting from cost pass-through. The case law that the FCC cited was not applicable to ISPs. Moreover, Section 251 itself directs the FCC to consider these impacts.[178]

Eight years later, the FCC's attitude remained unchanged. A commenter on the Open Internet IRFA stated that the IRFA was defective because the FCC had ineffectively followed the statutory requirements for a regulatory flexibility analysis, which were cited in the comment.[179] The FCC responded:

> [The commenter] does not provide any case law to support its interpretation that the Commission is in violation of these aspects of the statute, nor does [the commenter] attempt to argue that SBEs have actually or theoretically been harmed. Rather, [the commenter] is concerned that by not following its reading of these parts of the law, the Commission is being hypocritical by not being transparent enough.

Description and Estimate of the Number of Small Entities to Which the Actions Taken Will Apply

The FCC did its analysis of small entities at different levels of aggregation. In addition to analysis of six-digit NAICS industries, the FCC used subsets of businesses, which for our purposes will be called "industry groupings." These industry groupings were defined in terms of spectrum band(s) or of some combination of technology, type of service, and licensure.[180] At least some of these industry groupings were defined with reference to specific regulations or license auctions. The FCC, however, uses the same industry grouping definitions throughout all of its analyses.

The degree to which any regulation "will apply" and the nature or severity of impacts on any industry or industry grouping were very poorly defined at both the extensive and intensive margins.

- On one hand, it is not clear why many of the numerous – sometimes dozens and in one case 50 – industries and industry groupings were included in specific regulations. One regulation included Electric Power Generation, Transmission and Distribution;[181] another had 15 Computer and Electronic Product Manufacturing industries; and electronic retail and wholesale industries were included in one regulation. Similarly the reason for inclusion of specific industries and industry groupings within the Information sector was not clear. The only explanation was an occasional indication that the FCC wanted to include every industry grouping in which an entity to which the rule applied might be found.[182]
- On the other hand, the extent of applicability of a regulation or the severity of impact within industries or industry groupings were never mentioned.

The FCC's broad interpretation of "entities to which the actions taken will apply," which included many industries that were only indirectly affected, was incompatible with the FCC's position that only effects on directly regulated industries need to be considered in an analysis. In a number of places the FCC was quite explicit that it was including industries that it considered extraneous to any analysis - indicating that these estimates were not intended to be the basis for impact analysis.[183]

The FCC used several methodological approaches and several sources for both small-business size standards and data on businesses. Individually these methodologies are flawed – sometimes fatally. Collectively they produced estimates of such poor quality that the data were unfit for quantitative analysis.

First, at the most aggregate level, the FCC used data from the quinquennial Economic Census[184] together with the SBA size standards for six-digit NAICS industries. Using this approach, the FCC estimated numbers of small businesses in the industry. These NAICS industries were located both within the Publishing; Broadcasting; Telecommunications; and Data Processing, Hosting, and Related Services subsectors[185] and also in other sectors of the economy.[186] While Census data are the starting point for any impact analysis, this specific approach had two significant drawbacks.

- In some analyses, six-digit NAICS industries are so broad that most entities in it are irrelevant. In a rule establishing a new Medical Device Radiocommunication Service, for example, the FCC used data for:
  - Wireless communication equipment manufacturers (NAICS 334220),[187]
  - Wireless service providers (NAICS 517110), and
  - Public Safety Radio Services (licenses issued to all "small" governmental entities).
- For most industries in the Broadcasting and Telecommunications subsectors, the SBA size standards do not match the size categories in the Economic Census data. The FCC resorted to giving two numbers of entities, neither of which (nor the sum of which) fit the SBA size standard.[188] There are numerous ways to deal with this issue, including using Census data formatted at the SBA Advocacy's request. The FCC, however, did nothing more than report the numbers it found in the published Economic Census.

Most of the analyses of individual industries concluded with a statement to the effect that "the majority" or "the vast majority" of entities were small. This statement is almost meaningless, because – with the exception of a few specific niches (e.g., DBS Service) – the vast majority of entities in any industry are small.[189]

Second, the FCC used non-Census data on businesses size[190] in each industry grouping, together with the SBA size standard for the relevant NAICS industry. [191] This is the only approach that produced an actual point estimate of the number of small entities. The FCC sometimes repeated its "estimate" that a majority of entities affected by its action were small, even when it had price numbers (e.g., 31 out of 33 ISPs were small).

Third, for cable operations the FCC used subscriber-based size standards, which took advantage of the fact that it had subscription data. Thus the FCC utilized its own data on subscribers to estimate the numbers of:

- Cable companies, using a regulatory standard of 400,000 subscribers derived from 1992 Cable Act (47 CFR 76.901(e));
- Cable systems using a regulatory standard of 15,000 subscribers ((47 CFR 76.901(c)); and

- Cable system operators, using a hybrid standard of 667,000 subscribers[192] or $250 million in revenue based on the Communications Act of 1934.

In this case the FCC also estimated small cable businesses using Census data and the SBA standard for Cable and Other Subscription Programming (NAICS 515210). This multiple-estimate approach raised several issues:

- The FCC never attempted to resolve the conflict between estimates using SBA's revenue-based size standard and the subscription-based regulatory size standards.
- The FCC never clarified the relationship between cable system operators (on the one hand) and cable systems and cable operators (on the other).
- Potential affiliations among cable systems, cable operators, and cable system operators, which could have affected the size class of entities, were not explicitly addressed.

Fourth, the FCC used a count of licenses issued to each industry grouping, together with the SBA size standard for the relevant NAICS industry. This approach produced results in two cases where the number of licensees was very small, and FCC could identify each by size.[193] In a third case,[194] the FCC simply assumed that all non-educational licensees were small. In the other cases, the FCC lacked any real size data and estimated (or assumed) that "all," "almost all," or a number less than or equal to the total number of licensees were small.[195]

Fifth, the FCC based estimates of the number of small businesses on data from auctions for licenses, using FCC size standards for small businesses and very small businesses, which had been developed to determine eligibility for small-business provisions such as bidding credits in those auctions. The FCC reported auction results for:

- Auctions for which small was $40 million in revenue and very small was $15 million;[196]
- Auctions for which small was $15 million in revenue and very small was $3 million;[197] and
- Auctions for which the FCC did not report size standards.[198]

For each auction, the FCC reported the number of small firms that won licenses and (usually) the number of licenses they won. Sometimes the total number of winning bidders and/or total number of licenses won was also reported. The fundamental problem was that these results – even when reported for several auctions – provided only a fragmentary snapshot of small entities. Auction winners do not include incumbents that did not bid or win licenses in that auction. [199] As the FCC itself observed:

> we note that, as a general matter, the number of winning bidders that claim to qualify as small businesses at the close of an auction does not necessarily represent the number of small businesses currently in service.

Auction data covered a substantial time period, with some reported auctions occurring ten or more years before the analysis. The fact that different types of licenses might be included in the same auction[200] made interpretation of the data more difficult. In addition, the appropriateness of the auction size standards for regulatory flexibility analysis was questionable. The FCC repeatedly stated that the SBA had approved these size standards – only occasionally noting that this approval was for auction purposes. The $40 million FCC standard is much larger than any of the current SBA revenue standards ($7 million to $25 million), and in the one instance where both standards were quoted for the same industry grouping (Multichannel Multipoint Distributions Services), the FCC standard was $40 million, while the (2003) SBA standard was $12.5 million.

Finally, for a number of industry groupings, the FCC did not attempt to estimate the number of small businesses in an industry grouping, because it lacked the data for one of several reasons:

- The FCC had no revenue data,[201] generally because either:
  - Registration or licensing did not require financial information, or
  - No licensing was required.
- The FCC had no auction data reportedly because no auctions had been held, although there was an auction size standard;[202]
- No size standard had yet been set;[203] or
- SBA's size standard was defined in terms of annual output (4 million megawatt hours), and "Census data do not track electric output."[204]

The different estimation techniques produced data that had serious comparability problems of several types:

- Different data sources classify entities differently, so that the same entities may not be included in data from different sources. In general, Census classifications would include more entities than FCC licensees, so that one would expect Census data to produce larger numbers than license data, subscription data, or other FCC data that probably use narrower definitions.
- FCC auction size standards are set at higher revenue levels than SBA's revenue size standards, so that results using the two standards were not comparable.
- Similarly, the FCC applied different subscription size standards, as well as an SBA revenue standard, to cable entities.
- The FCC tended to mix revenue-based and employment-based size standards in ways that produced non-comparable results. This occured with:
  - NAICS industries with employment size standards and industry groupings within them that estimated with auction data,
  - Closely related industry groupings,[205] and
  - Even the same industry grouping.[206]
- Auction data were so different from any of the other data that it was not possible even to perform any mathematical operation across the entire set of data.

Double-counting – even triple-counting - was rampant in the data. This occurred in a number of different ways:

- All of the industry groupings are within one of the six-digit NAICS industries that were discussed. When entities at both levels were enumerated,[207] double-counting was inevitable.
- Some analyses counted the same six-digit NAICS industry twice.[208]
- Use of multiple subscription standards counted cable establishments twice – three times including the estimates based on SBA size standards and census data.
- There may be additional double-counting if industry groupings overlap (principally a concern for groupings defined by spectrum band and in other terms), but this is not clear.

The analyses reviewed show an inconsistent pattern in updating the data over time, as new data become available.

- There were numerous examples of old data being cited:
    - Analyses in 2007 and 2010 cited 1992 data on small municipal governments,
    - An analysis in 2004 used data for SIC industries,
    - In the Preserving Open Internet FRFA (September, 2011), 2002 Census data were used for Satellite Telecommunications and for Cable and Other Program Distribution, although 2007 Census data were used for other industries,
    - Auction data five or ten years old – and even older – were often cited (although relatively recent auctions sometimes were added in),
    - A 2007 analysis used 1994 Private Land Mobile Radio data, and
    - A 2003 analysis used 1995 cable subscription data.
- There also was apparent confusion when NAICS definitions changed. In 2011, for example, the FCC put wireless firms under Wireless Communication Services (except Satellite) instead of the "now-superseded categories of 'Paging' and 'Cellular and Other Wireless Communications'" that it had previously used. In fact, those categories continue to exist – as seven-digit NAICS industries.[209]

The FCC took little or no initiative to identify data beyond six digit Economic Census data and in-house data that it routinely collected. With one possible exception, the FCC did not use more detailed Census data[210] to get a better fit with its own industry groupings, nor did the FCC use alternative forms of Census data to match SBA size thresholds or get more detail on the size distribution of entities within an industry.[211] Except occasionally for wireline industry groupings,[212] the FCC made no use of industry data. Instead, the FCC used inferior techniques such as auction data or relied on assumptions. Moreover, the state of understanding of an industry never advanced.[213]

The FCC routinely cited independent ownership as part of the definition of small entity, but it virtually never looked into whether entities were affiliated. TV translator stations and TV booster stations, for example, are affiliates of larger entities almost by definition. Yet on two occasions when they appeared in the analyses (along with Class A stations and low power television stations), the FCC concluded, "given the nature of these services, we will presume that these licensees qualify as small entities under the SBA definition." In a third – earlier - rule the FCC opined "that most, if not all, of these" could be classified as small and did "recognize that most... are owned by a parent station which, in some cases, would" not meet SBA's standard for small.

The FCC analyses had a characteristic not found in any other agency's work. Not only were the industry groupings consistently defined for all the analyses, virtually the same text recurred in analysis after analysis – sometimes with a sentence or two rephrased and sometimes with newer data, but not with any substantive change. Each FCC regulatory flexibility analysis was a set of cut-and-paste jobs - or direct copies - from previous analyses. This style doubtless facilitated assembling estimates of entities to which the rule would apply, but it entirely precluded any discussion of impacts – much less nuances about the extent and severity of impacts.

Over the period reviewed, lack of coherent data on small entities affected made it impossible for the FCC to perform impact analysis or regulatory flexibility analysis. Conversely, the FCC was on record as saying that no impact analysis was required, and so it did nothing to improve the quality of the data.

Description of Projected Reporting, Recordkeeping, and Other Compliance Requirements

The FCC's discussions of compliance requirements focused almost entirely on reporting and recordkeeping requirements. A majority of analyses provided lists of filing, reporting, or other information requirements – what information was required and in what circumstances. Some of these were very specific;[214] more often they were general and vague;[215] and occasionally entirely uninformative.[216] A majority of analyses referred to existing forms and procedures. In some of these cases the only requirements mentioned involved using existing forms or procedures in new contexts. One rule provided instructions for filling out a petition form. Some requirements entailed complying with some existing rule.[217] In four cases the FCC reported that there would be no change in current practice, no increase in reporting and recordkeeping requirements, or reductions in requirements were described.[218]

The Triennial Review Order took recapping the substance of the rule to an entirely new level. After stating "we adopt rules to implement a congressionally-mandated scheme," the FCC spelled out its conclusions about "the necessary and impair standards of section 251(d)(2)."[219] The discussion did not provide a sense of what these requirements would entail operationally, and the focus was on actions to be taken by large ILECs.

In the Open Internet rule, requirements were summarized as relatively modest web site changes[220] that did not have significant professional skills requirements.[221] The FCC initially stated that "we do not require additional forms of disclosure" but then added that it might require additional disclosures to the Commission. The FCC's somewhat self-contradictory discussion provided no sense of the scope of the rule's impacts.

The FCC appears to have interpreted compliance requirements in a very limited way – including only the compliance activities specifically named in the RFA. "Other Compliance Requirements" is meant to include a wide range of other types of compliance activities by small entities that incur costs. Examples of such activities might include actions and replacement of obsolete equipment required by migration from one frequency to another, activities required as part of participation in the DTV consumer education campaign, and operational changes required by rule changes. The discussions seem incomplete, and they provide little or no basis for estimation or understanding of costs.

Steps Taken to Minimize Significant Economic Impact on Small Entities, and Significant Alternatives Considered

The FCC customarily cited the classes of regulatory flexibility alternatives listed in the RFA. The ensuing discussions, however, did not follow this outline or emphasize small businesses. The purposes and benefits of the regulation were reviewed in a number of cases – often with the benefits being given rather enthusiastic treatment. Most rules involved some element of flexibility, but these elements tended to be noted in hindsight, and some were inherent in the rule. Several mentioned (in discussion compliance requirements) that a form or provision was not mandatory. Twelve rules included substantive discussions.[222]

- In seven rules, benefits were cited, with "including small entities" as the sole reference to small businesses.[223]
- In three rules, benefits for small entities that were inherent in the structure of the rule were cited, although some of these pertained to new entrants rather than incumbents.[224]
- Two rules included measures that were explicitly designed for small entities:
  - In one rule, measures were adopted in response to public comments.[225]
  - The Triennial Review Order included several provisions that appeared to be relatively minor tweaks of the rule.[226]

The Triennial Review Order was unusual in that the impact on small entities due to the degree and nature of unbundling of network elements was a central issue in the regulation. This issue was summarized in the concept of an "impairment," whose linguistic root is statutory.[227] The FCC parsed the network elements in its impairment analysis, which used a "granular approach, including the considerations of customer class, geography, and service." Most of the discussion under the heading Steps Taken to Minimize Significant Economic Impact on Small Entities in the Order FRFA was about this approach and the results it produced. Some "least burdensome... alternatives" were eventually listed (see above), but the only other discussion of alternatives was a list of those suggested by commenters that the FCCV had rejected. Most of this discussion was abstract. For example:

> We have considered the resources and needs of various carriers, including small businesses, and have examined the state of the marketplace to determine whether it was economically feasible for competitors to self-provision network elements or obtain them from competitive sources other than incumbent LECs. We believe this approach strikes the appropriate balance between the needs of competitors – including small competitors – to access certain network elements, against the burdens unbundling imposes upon incumbent LECs.

The FRFA for the Order on Remand was considerably more focused on alternatives. Where small entities were involved, however, the choice of alternatives often hinged on a concept such as "reasonable inferences" or "reasonably efficient competitor."[228] In most instances, the discussion either contained an acknowledgement of adverse impacts on small entities,[229] or it was a rejection of comments of, or alternatives sought by, a small entities. Alternatives designed to minimize impacts on small entities were absent.

The FCC has some standing accommodations for small entities, such as auction preferences. The size of the licensee is an integral part of some aspects of rules, such as service area size. Here the FCC appears to consider small entities. Otherwise, there were no signs that the FCC developed and adopted rules for the purpose of minimizing impacts on small entities.

Assessment

The FCC does not perform impact analysis or regulatory flexibility analysis as it is prescribed by the RFA and described in SBA.[230] The FCC stated that it complied with the RFA "fully" and "precisely." The analyses reviewed presented quite a different picture.

- The ongoing series of orders associated with many dockets and rulemakings produce an evolving set of impacts and a shifting baseline that would require repeated revision.
- Notices of proposed rulemaking lacked proposed rules.
- For any given regulation, the FCC compiled a set of industries "to which the actions taken will apply" that was designed "to achieve a fuller record." This set of industries was too broadly defined for impact analysis, and the extent and severity of impacts within any industry were never described.
- The FCC's estimates of the numbers of small entities almost always stopped short of anything useful. They used heterogeneous methodologies that resulted in problems of comparability, overage, double-counting, and other issues that were never resolved. Consequently, it was not possible to perform an impact analysis with the resulting data set.
- The FCC recycled boilerplate text in its discussions of entities – text that did not differ substantively (except for occasional data updates) across rules or over time. This precluded any regulation-specific information and thus any impact analysis.
- The FCC did not collect quantitative data on impacts. The discussions of compliance requirements were almost entirely limited to paperwork (reporting and recordkeeping) requirements and restatement of the provisions of the regulation.
- The discussion of Steps Taken to Minimize Impacts usually did not include alternatives designed for small entities, and small entities often were mentioned only incidentally.
- When challenged in comments that it had not performed an impact analysis or fulfilled other procedural requirements, the FCC denied that it is required to perform an impact analysis as part of the RFA and otherwise disputed the comments.

The empirical analysis of impacts of rules and alternative provisions, which lies at the heart of regulatory flexibility analysis, was consistently absent in the FCC regulations reviewed.

It appears that the FCC's failure to analyze may not be limited to regulatory flexibility analysis. In *U.S. Telecom Association*, the court decision to which the Triennial Review Order was responding, the court repeatedly criticized the FCC for failing to provide empirical support for its case. This failure was a decisive factor in the court's ruling against the FCC and indirectly in the substance of the Triennial Review Order. Excerpts from the decision[231] provide illustration:

> Because the Commission has loftily abstracted away all specific markets, and because its concept of impairing cost-differentials is so broad... we have no way of assessing the real meaning of that conclusion.
> The Commission appears simply to assume that any such rule would be unpredictable and hard to apply.
> In the end, then, the entire argument about expanding competition and investment boils down to the Commission's expression of its belief that in this area more unbundling is better.
> Because the Commission's concept of "impairing" cost disparities is so broad and unrooted in any analysis of the competing values at stake in implementation of the Act, we cannot uphold even the two non-universal mandates adopted by the Commission.

The actual consequences of a regulation are usually poorly understood because retroactive analysis of outcomes is infrequently done. While it is not the objective of this study to do such analysis, the Triennial Review Order was long enough ago that data are readily available. Economic Census data for the ISP industry show that:

- In 1997 there were 2,751 ISPs.
- In 2002, after five years of the FCC's original regulatory scheme, there were 4,379 ISPs.
- In 2007, after the 2003 Triennial Review Order, there were 3,013 ISPs.

That is the magnitude of the impact that the FCC refused to look for.

5. Federal Deposit Insurance Corporation

Overview

The Federal Deposit Insurance Corporation (FDIC)[232] is an independent agency created by the Congress to maintain stability and public confidence in the nation's financial system by insuring deposits in banks and thrift institutions for at least $250,000; by identifying, monitoring and addressing risks to the deposit insurance funds; and by limiting the effect on the economy and the financial system when a bank or thrift institution fails.

An independent agency of the federal government, the FDIC was created in 1933 in response to the thousands of bank failures that occurred in the 1920s and early 1930s. The FDIC receives no Congressional appropriations – it is funded by premiums that banks and thrift institutions pay for deposit insurance coverage and from earnings on investments in U.S. Treasury securities.

The standard insurance amount is $250,000 per depositor, per insured bank, for each account ownership category. The FDIC insures deposits only. It does not insure securities, mutual funds or similar types of investments that banks and thrift institutions may offer.

The FDIC directly examines and supervises more than 4,900 banks and savings banks for operational safety and soundness, more than half of the institutions in the banking system. The FDIC is the primary federal regulator of banks that are chartered by the states that do not join the Federal Reserve System. In addition, the FDIC is the back-up supervisor for the remaining insured banks and thrift institutions.

The FDIC also examines banks for compliance with consumer protection laws, including the Fair Credit Billing Act, the Fair Credit Reporting Act, the Truth-In-Lending Act, and the Fair Debt Collection Practices Act, to name a few. Finally, the FDIC examines banks for compliance with the Community Reinvestment Act (CRA) which requires banks to help meet the credit needs of the communities they were chartered to serve.

To protect insured depositors, the FDIC responds immediately when a bank or thrift institution fails. Institutions generally are closed by their chartering authority – the state regulator, the Office of the Comptroller of the Currency, or the Office of Thrift Supervision. The FDIC has several options for resolving institution failures, but the one most used is to sell deposits and loans of the failed institution to another institution. Customers of the failed institution automatically become customers of the assuming institution. Most of the time, the transition is seamless from the customer's point of view.

Regulations
The FDIC promulgated 20 distinct[233] rules in the study period. Seven of these were joint rules with other regulatory agencies. Most of the rules involved incremental changes to the existing regulatory structure, and most rules were promulgated in direct response to changes in statutes or the financial environment. None involved identifiable significant small-entity impacts.

- Three rules concerned assessments for the Deposit Insurance Fund and were made directly or indirectly in response to the recent financial crisis.
  - One raised the designated reserve ratio to provide better protection against future crises,[234]
  - One mandated prepaid assessments to deal with a current liquidity shortage,[235] and
  - One implemented provisions of the Dodd-Frank Act.[236]
- Two rules made technical changes in regulations to incorporate a statutory increase in the standard maximum deposit insurance amount (SMDIA) from $100,000 to $250,000. Congress first extended a temporary increase in SMDIA and then made in permanent.[237]
- Four joint rules amended Community Reinvestment Act regulations of the agencies involved.[238]
  - Two expanded the range of activities by banking institutions that agencies were required to consider in making CRA assessments,[239] and
  - Two made annual CPI-based adjustments to the definitions of "small" and "intermediate" institutions used in the agencies' CRA performance standards.[240]
- Two rules made changes in deposit insurance regulations in response to changes in the generally accepted accounting principles (GAPP).
  - One joint rule excluded or limited some practices involving consolidation of institutions and transfer of assets,[241] and
  - One provided temporary grandfathering of a safe harbor provision for securitizations.[242]
- Four rules implemented the provisions of recent statutory changes.
  - Two provided unlimited coverage for noninterest-bearing accounts, in accordance with the Dodd-Frank Act,[243]
  - One joint rule developed and adopted a model privacy notification form, in accordance with the Gramm-Leach-Bliley Act,[244] and
  - One joint rule set registration requirements for financial institution employees who originate mortgages and oversight requirements for their employers, under the Secure and Fair Enforcement for Mortgage (S.A.F.E.) Licensing Act.[245]
- One rule provided an option involving deduction goodwill from type 1 capital.[246]
- Four rules involved what were essentially housekeeping matters.

- One rule amended interest rate restriction regulations by revising and clarifying some definitions that had become obsolete,[247]
- One rule incorporated – by cross-reference – recent Securities and Exchange Commission regulations,[248]
- One rule modified risk-based capital guidelines to remove disincentives to participate in HUD's Making Home Affordable Program,[249] and
- One rule implemented Dodd-Frank Act provisions concerning the FDIC's role as receiver of a failing major financial company.[250]

Analysis

Regulatory Flexibility Analysis

Exemption

Three rules were exempt from the RFA because they did not require a NPRM. That is appropriate, as two of these rules updated definitions and the third incorporated SEC regulations by reference.

Three rules pertained to Deposit Insurance Fund assessments. The FDIC stated that these rules were exempt from the RFA by definition.[251]

- In one of these rules the FDIC then proceeded to provide the number of small entities affected, estimate compliance costs for small entities, and provide a benchmark[252] to determine that the impacts were small.
- In another rule, the FDIC explained how the impacts were strictly proportional to institution size.
- In the third, the FDIC estimated that small institutions would benefit from reduced assessments.

The overall effect of these rules was significantly to lower small institutions' share of assessments. This effect stemmed from the third of these rules, which rebalanced the assessment base, rates, and schedules in accordance with recent loss experience – and large banks had been the major source of hits on the Deposit insurance fund.

Certification

All but one of the other FDIC regulations had no more than an initial regulatory flexibility analyses. They concluded with a certification that there will not be a significant impact on a substantial number of small entities.

Explanations or analyses – although quite basic - adequately supported this conclusion.

Five rules made no real change in requirements, merely provided clarification, or slightly simplified requirements. The FDIC provided concise explanation as to why there are no impacts.[253]

Five rules were not mandatory, and the FDIC opined that small financial institutions may benefit by taking advantage of the rule.

- Three rules expand the CRA consideration options for financial institutions or ease regulations for participation in a HUD program.
- One joint rule created a model privacy notification form.
- One rule pertained to deduction of goodwill.

Three rules did not have adverse impacts on small banking institutions for various reasons:

- One rule applied to complex financial transactions, which the FDIC believed small banking organizations rarely – if ever participated in.
- One rule clarified rules and procedures for FDIC employees.
- One rule created non-trivial savings in assessments for small banking organizations participating in an FDIC program that was being supplanted.

The rule implementing the S.A.F.E. Mortgage Licensing Act, which was jointly promulgated by six agencies, imposed costs far greater than any other of these regulations. The rule required registration of financial institution employees who act as a residential mortgage loan originators and oversight by their employees. There was a *de minimis* exception for employees,[254] and (by extension) for financial institutions, although institutions with no registered employees still incurred some monitoring and procedural costs. The FDIC did its most careful job here. Compliance costs were estimated based on labor hours and costs. The FDIC estimated costs for the 861 small banks subject to the full regulation and for the 2,255 small banks subject to *de minimis* provisions, and the FDIC distinguished between start-up costs and annual costs thereafter. This was a more detailed analysis than was published by any other agency. Compliance costs were then compared to the institutions' total non-interest costs and were found to be non-significant (0.7 percent in the first year and 0.3 percent thereafter in the full-requirements scenario).[255]

Regulatory Flexibility Alternatives

There was little consideration of regulatory flexibility alternatives as such in most of these rulemakings. The lack of significant impact of the rule on small entities was a factor in many cases. A number of specific factors mitigated against regulatory flexibility alternatives.

- For some rules, there really were no alternatives.[256]
- Some rules did little more than clarify existing regulations.
- In some cases, alternatives were constrained by terms of the enabling statute.[257]

Some of the rules implicitly involved regulatory flexibility alternatives, although they were not necessarily described as such prior to the regulatory flexibility analysis. Some rules were not mandatory.[258] Some rules had, in effect, a small business exemption. A change in the assessment schedule had a proportionately larger impact on large banks, part of one rule applied only to large banks, and another regulated actions practiced almost exclusively by large banks. This is rather natural; practices of large banks have been the source of recent financial turmoil, and one should expect regulations to focus on them.

The rule implementing the S.A.F.E. Mortgage Licensing Act, which had the largest impacts, also had the most explicit consideration of regulatory flexibility. This included a *de minimis* provision and general policy development requirements that were essentially performance-based and adaptable to different sizes of institutions. As this was a joint rule, however, the regulatory flexibility cannot be attributed to any one agency.

Assessment

For a variety of reasons, the FDIC did not have to go beyond an initial regulatory flexibility analysis. The FDIC explained basis for the certifications clearly. Even in rules that were exempt from the RFA, the FDIC discussed effects on small entities, rather than simply asserting the exemption. In the one case where substantial analysis was required to support the certification - the S.A.F.E. Mortgage Licensing Act rule - the FDIC did a very craftsman-like job. Although it is not clear how much of a role the FDIC played in developing them, the rule incorporated significant regulatory flexibility alternatives.

6. Federal Election Commission

Overview

The Federal Election Commission (FEC)[259] is the independent regulatory agency charged with administering and enforcing the Federal Election Campaign Act (FECA), the statute that governs the financing of federal elections. The FEC has jurisdiction over the financing of campaigns for the U.S. House, the U.S. Senate, the Presidency and the Vice Presidency. The duties of the FEC are to:

- Ensure public disclosure of funds raised and spent to influence federal elections;
- Enforce limitations and prohibitions on contributions and expenditures made to influence federal elections; and
- Oversee the public financing of Presidential campaigns and administer the Presidential Campaign Fund, which provides public funds to candidates for president and nominating conventions.

The Commission clarifies the FECA and the public funding statutes through regulations, codified in Title 11 of the Code of Federal Regulations.

Regulations

The Federal Election Commission had no regulations listed in the Spring 2010, Fall 2010, or Spring 2011 Unified Agenda as "Final Rule Stage" or "Completed Action." Thus no further analysis was done on FEC regulations.

7. Federal Energy Regulatory Commission

Overview

The Federal Energy Regulatory Commission (FERC)[260] is an independent agency that regulates the interstate transmission of electricity, natural gas, and oil. FERC also reviews proposals to build liquefied natural gas (LNG) terminals and interstate natural gas pipelines as well as licensing hydropower projects. FERC's mission is to assist consumers in obtaining reliable, efficient and sustainable energy services at a reasonable cost through appropriate regulatory and market means. As part of that mission, FERC:

- Regulates the transmission and wholesale sales of electricity in interstate commerce;[261]
- Protects the reliability of the high voltage interstate transmission system through mandatory reliability standards;
- Reviews the siting application for electric transmission projects under limited circumstances;
- Licenses and inspects private, municipal, and state hydroelectric projects;
- Reviews certain mergers and acquisitions and corporate transactions by electricity companies;
- Regulates the transmission and sale of natural gas for resale in interstate commerce;
- Approves the siting and abandonment of interstate natural gas pipelines and storage facilities;
- Ensures the safe operation and reliability of proposed and operating LNG terminals;
- Regulates the transportation of oil by pipeline in interstate commerce;[262]
- Monitors and investigates energy markets;
- Oversees environmental matters related to natural gas and hydroelectricity projects and other matters;
- Administers accounting and financial reporting regulations and conduct of regulated companies; and
- Enforces FERC regulatory requirements through imposition of civil penalties and other means.

FERC does not have jurisdiction over local distribution and retail sale of electricity and gas, which fall under state public utility commissions, or over local facilities, except to the extent that the interstate system may be affected.

The Energy Policy Act of 2005 gave FERC additional responsibilities in the form of initiatives, including:

- **Smart Grid.** Applying digital technologies to the grid, and enabling real-time coordination of information from generation supply resources, demand resources, and distributed energy resources (DER);
- **Demand Response.** Assessing of demand response potential and to developing a national action plan on demand response; and

- **Integration of Renewables.** Allowing all resources, including renewable energy resources, to compete in jurisdictional markets on a level playing field.

Regulations

FERC published 31 final rules that were included in the Unified Agenda in the study period. Of these rules:

- Seven rules dealt with matters that were internal to the Commission;[263]
- Six rules dealt with mandatory reliability standards for the national or a regional transmission grid, which were developed by the North American Electric Reliability Corporation (NERC).[264]
- Six rules involved updating fees, cost limits, or interest rates;[265]
- One rule provided a cost methodology;[266]
- Four rules mandated adoption of consensus business practices standards by the
  - Wholesale Gas Quadrant of the North American Energy Standards Board (2 rules) or the
  - Wholesale Electric Quadrant of the North American Energy Standards Board (2 rules);[267]
- Three rules affected posting, reporting, or filing requirements for natural gas companies;[268]
- Three rules were designed to increase the efficiency of energy markets;[269]
- One rule eased restrictions on access to critical energy infrastructure information;[270]
- One rule revised certification of qualifying status for a small power production or cogeneration facility;[271] and
- One rule mandated reliability standards for critical infrastructure protection.[272]

Analysis

Regulatory Flexibility Analysis

FERC did not perform complete formal regulatory flexibility analysis. In most cases the FERC either certified that the rule would not have a significant economic impact on a substantial number of small entities or cited an exemption from the RFA. In a number of cases, however, FERC also discussed some type of measures to reduce burdens. A number of factors contributed to the certification.

No Notice of Proposed Rulemaking

Thirteen of the rules did not have or require an NOPR.[273] Rules that do not require an NOPR are exempt from RFA requirements. Many of these concerned matters of "internal agency procedure" or "a ministerial correction."

Demographics of the Regulation Population

FERC's jurisdiction does not generally include companies that operate only within one state. Very few interstate energy companies, which include electric power transmission and pipelines, are small. FERC consistently cited data that only six small electric companies (out of a total of about 130) and four small gas companies (out of a total of 125) under its jurisdiction meet the SBA definition of "small."[274] As one notice put it succinctly, "The Commission does not consider this [4 or 6] a substantial number." That line of reasoning applies to about half of FERC rules reviewed.[275]

In several of these rules, the regulated population was a subset of all electric transmission companies or gas companies, and this subset included fewer (if any) small entities. Examples included:

- Holding companies of public utilities and/or natural gas companies;
- Regional transmission organizations (RTOs) and independent system operators (ISOs);
- Utilities participating in a Bonneville Power Administration program; and
- The Western Interconnection (the area of the Western Electricity Coordinating Council).

In one rule,[276] a commenter suggested that the FERC regulation would apply to a large number of retail entities and their regulators. FERC took the opportunity to buttress its interpretation of "substantial" – and to clarify that entities regulated by a state authority do not count – by citing two court decisions:

> In *Mid-Tex*, the court accepted the Commission's conclusion that, since virtually all of the public utilities that it regulates do not fall within the meaning of the term "small entities" as defined in the RFA, the Commission did not need to prepare a regulatory flexibility analysis in connection with its proposed rule.

In... *American Trucking Associations, Inc. v. EPA*, the U.S. Court of Appeals for the District of Columbia... found that because the states, not EPA, had the direct authority to impose the burden on small entities, EPA's regulation did not have a direct impact on small entities.

Regulations Affecting Small Entities

Two of the FERC regulations did affect substantial numbers of small entities. In both cases, the FERC discussed measures that it had built into the rule to reduce the burden on small entities.

A rule on certification of qualifying facility status for a small power production or cogeneration facility (QFs) replaced an existing form with an electronic version. The FERC identified three types of regulatory changes that the rule made to minimize burdens:

- New information requirements were kept to a minimum to include: Geographical coordinates – only if the facility had no street address, and Information to determine applicability of EPAct 2005 cogeneration requirements.
- The form was clarified, streamlined, and accompanied by step-by-step instructions. The FERC believed that this was easier to complete than the old form and also "should substantially reduce the burden of complying with EPAct 2005 cogeneration requirements."
- Facilities with 1 MW capacity or less were exempt from electronic filing.

The Critical Infrastructure Protection (CIP) Standards require "certain users, owners, and operators of the Bulk-Power System" to take measures to safeguard critical cyber assets.[277] For this purpose, FERC's jurisdiction extended to all the local utilities – many of them small - that would normally not concern it. FERC estimated that 632 small utilities (almost all of them municipalities and cooperatives) would be affected.

Like other reliability standards, CIP entailed registration with the ERO.[278] Registration itself was subject to size thresholds.[279] This rule also contained a criterion that the Commission-certified electric reliability organization (ERO) make a determination that a specific small entity has a material impact on the Bulk-Power System. In another rule in the same time frame, FERC adopted a variant definition of bulk-power system "which [FERC believed, would] reduce significantly the number of small utilities responsible for compliance with mandatory Reliability Standards."[280]

Provisions of the regulation included a sort of tiering. The initial issue for a utility is whether it has a critical cyber asset. All registered utilities having a material impact on the Bulk-Power System would have to determine this. FERC estimated that complying with the initial identification standard would be a relatively minor cost, and a registered entity that did not identify any critical cyber assets would have no further compliance obligations.

Utilities that did identify critical cyber assets "would have to expend significant amounts of resources on labor and technology to comply with the CIP Reliability Standards."[281] FERC suggested two approaches to mitigating these costs:

- FERC noted that "small entities could choose to collectively select a single consultant to develop model software and programs to comply with the CIP Reliability Standards on their behalf [which] could significantly reduce the costs that would be incurred if each company would address these issues independently."
- FERC "also noted that small entities could join a joint action agency or similar organization, which could accept responsibility for compliance with mandatory Reliability Standards on behalf of its members and also may divide the responsibility for compliance with its members."

Several commenters expressed concern about impacts on small entities and questioned whether FERC had paid enough attention to supporting compliance by small entities. Several commenters made suggestions, which the FERC discussed but generally did not adopt – believing that the suggestions were out of scope, did not contribute more than the options suggested, or could create vulnerabilities. FERC directed the ERO to address some concerns through the Reliability Systems development process and to develop guidance for compliance and provide information that would be helpful.

FERC reaffirmed its certification that the rule would not have a significant impact on a substantial number of small entities. It is not clear how the FERC could determine that a substantial number of entities would have to proceed beyond the identification standard, but the FERC may well have made as many accommodations as a full regulatory flexibility analysis would have produced.

Assessment

The interstate nature of the industry that the FERC regulates results in very few small entities being under FERC jurisdiction for most rules. The FERC did not usually take regulatory flexibility analysis beyond the automatic certification stage. When it did it showed a reasonable understanding of the numbers of small entities affected – if not a precise industry profile – and a good enough understanding of impacts to be able to develop and consider alternative measures. Electronic filing is an example. For most businesses, this is likely to represent an efficiency, but some (generally very small) entities do not have the capacity, which the FERC acknowledged. Measures such as alternative reporting options, thresholds and waivers also appeared in other regulations, suggesting that the FERC was mindful of their value. In the one case where impacts on small entities were significant, the FERC also left the door open for possible further burden reduction. The ability to apply regulatory flexibility principles that it usually does not need speaks well of the FERC.

8. Federal Housing Finance Agency

Overview

The Federal Housing Finance Agency (FHFA) is a new agency created by the Housing and Economic Recovery Act of 2008. FHFA's mission is to provide effective supervision, regulation and housing mission oversight of government-sponsored enterprises in the secondary mortgage markets (GSEs) – the Federal Home Loan Mortgage Corporation (Fannie Mae), the Federal National Mortgage Association (Freddie Mac), and the 12 Federal Home Loan Banks. The Housing and Economic Recovery Act combined the staffs and consolidated the power and regulatory authority of:

- The Office of Federal Housing Enterprise Oversight (OFHEO), whose regulations address capital standards and limitations on the assets, activities, and risk exposures of the two housing GSEs.
- The Federal Housing Finance Board (FHFB), which had regulatory oversight over the Federal Home Loan Banks, and
- The GSE mission office at the Department of Housing and Urban Development (HUD).

Regulations

During the study period, the FMC promulgated 17 final rules that were listed in the Unified Agenda. All of these directly affected some or all of the GSEs:

- Five rules pertained to integrating the Federal Housing Finance Board into the FHFA.[282]
- Two rules set financial requirements for the GSEs;[283]
- Six rules involved management, procedures, and policies of the GSEs;[284] and
- Four rules concerned programs, goals, and procedures of the Federal Home Loan Banks.[285]

Analysis

Regulatory Flexibility Analysis

In 15 of the rules, the FHFA certified categorically that the rule would not have a significant economic impact on a substantial number of small businesses. In almost all of these cases, the basis for the certification was the fact that Fannie Mae, Freddie Mac, and Federal Home Loan Banks "do not come within the meaning of small entities" as defined in, or for purposes of, the Regulatory Flexibility Act. Certification was automatic.

In two rules, the FHFA hedged slightly, saying that the rule was "not likely" to have such an effect. In these notices, the FHFA identified some entities beyond the agencies that might be affected but stated that their number was "not... substantial" or "limited." The circumstances of the cases suggest that there would not have been significant adverse impacts either:

- The *Equal Access to Justice Act* rule to established procedures for the submission and consideration of applications for awards of fees and other expenses by prevailing parties in adjudications against FHFA. There are not many such parties, and the procedures likely benefitted them.
- The *Debt Collection Act* rule affected persons or entities that owed debts to the FHFA (or some other agency). Payment of debt and related expenses are not normally considered impacts for purposes of regulatory analysis.

Assessment

The FHFA is essentially exempt from the RFA and made no significant attempt to do analysis beyond a boilerplate certification. The FHFA did, however, manage to note instances where their rules would have direct effects on some non-federal entities. In these cases, it refrained from using its boilerplate certification and at least considered whether the numbers of entities involved were small.

9. Federal Maritime Commission

Overview

The Federal Maritime Commission (FMC) is an independent regulatory agency responsible for the regulation of oceanborne transportation in the foreign commerce of the U.S. The Federal Maritime Commission:

- Monitors activities of ocean common carriers, marine terminal operators, conferences, ports, and ocean transportation intermediaries (OTIs) who operate in the U.S. foreign commerce to ensure they maintain just and reasonable practices, and oversees the financial responsibility of passenger vessel operators;
- Maintains a trade monitoring and enforcement program designed to assist regulated entities in achieving compliance, and to detect and appropriately remedy malpractices and violations set forth in section 10 of the Shipping Act;
- Monitors the laws and practices of foreign governments which could have a discriminatory or otherwise adverse impact on shipping conditions in the U.S;
- Enforces special regulatory requirements applicable to ocean common carriers owned or controlled by foreign governments (controlled carriers);
- Processes and reviews agreements and service contracts;
- Reviews common carriers' privately published tariff systems for accessibility and accuracy;
- Issues licenses to qualified OTIs in the U.S. and ensures all maintain evidence of financial responsibility; and
- Ensures passenger vessel operators demonstrate adequate financial responsibility for casualty and non-performance.

Regulations

During the study period, the FMC promulgated five final rules, one of which concluded a long-term action.

- Three rules were exempt from the APA notice and comment requirements – and had no NOPR – because they pertained to FMC management structure,[286] security of sensitive agency information,[287] and other agency practices and procedures.[288]
- One rule repealed an exemption from a statutory waiting period after filing a marine terminal agreement (MTA) out of concern that the immediate anti-trust immunity the exemption granted could have anticompetitive consequences.[289]
- One rule marked the end of a long-term action concerning Japanese port restrictions and requirements. The FMC had adopted a rule imposing countervailing costs, which was subsequently withdrawn in favor of reporting requirements on five oceangoing common carriers (two American and three Japanese).[290]

Analysis

Regulatory Flexibility Analysis

These rules did not raise significant regulatory flexibility issues; all were either exempt or had a virtually automatic certification. In most cases, however, the FMC did not make even these easy points.

- In the MTA rule, the FMC certified that there would not be a significant impact on a substantial number of small businesses because the regulated entities that would be affected – marine terminal operators and ocean common carriers – did not qualify as small under SBA guidelines.
- In the port restrictions rule, the FMC made no such certification, although it was entirely clear that only large ocean carriers were affected.
- In the three rules that were exempt from the RFA, the FMC did not bring up the RFA or mention the exemption.

Assessment

The FMC is lax in tying up the loose ends of regulatory flexibility analysis. This may be from lack of practice in cases where attention to detail and analytical procedure really matter. If marine terminal operators and ocean common carriers (some of them foreign) are all large, it appears that a considerable majority of the FMC's regulations may not require much RFA scrutiny.

10. Federal Mine Safety and Health Review Commission

Overview

The Federal Mine Safety and Health Review Commission (FMSHRC) is an independent adjudicative federal agency that provides administrative trial and appellate review of legal disputes arising under the Mine Act of 1977. Under the Mine Act, the U.S. Department of Labor issues regulations covering health and safety in the nation's mines. Mine Safety and Health Administration (MSHA) mine inspectors enforce these regulations by issuing citations and orders to mine operators.

The FMSHRC is an not a federal court; was established as an independent agency to ensure its impartiality in providing administrative review of MSHA's actions. The FMSHRC functions much like a court, however, and issues decisions – including determinations of appropriate penalties - after trial-like hearings conducted by FMSHRC administrative law judges. Certain FMSHRC ALJ decisions are reviewed by the Review Commission. Decisions of the Review Commission can be appealed to the United States Court of Appeals.

Regulations

The Mine Safety and Health Administration's regulations are codified in Title 30 of the Code of Federal Regulations, Part 1 to 199. The FMSHRC itself does not regulate mining or enforce the Mine Act. It is concerned solely with the adjudication of disputes under the Mine Act.

11. Federal Reserve System

Overview

Structure

The Federal Reserve System,[291] which was created by the Federal Reserve Act in 1913, is an unusual mixture of public and private elements.

Board of Governors

The Board of Governors, which is the national component of the Federal Reserve System, provides the leadership for the System. Guiding monetary policy action and analyzing domestic and international economic and financial conditions are among the responsibilities of the Board. The Board's most important responsibility is participating in the Federal Open Market Committee (FOMC), which conducts our nation's monetary policy

The Board also exercises broad supervisory control over the financial services industry, administers certain consumer protection regulations, and oversees the nation's payments system. The Board oversees the activities of Reserve Banks, sets reserve requirements for depository institutions, and approves changes in discount rates recommended by Reserve Banks.

Federal Reserve Banks

A network of 12 regional Federal Reserve Banks and 25 branches make up the Federal Reserve System under the general oversight of the Board of Governors. Reserve Banks are the operating arms of the central bank - serving banks, the U.S. Treasury, and, indirectly, the public. A Reserve Bank is often called a "banker's bank," storing currency and coin, and processing checks and electronic payments. Reserve Banks supervise commercial banks in their regions. They also handle the Treasury's payments, sell government securities and assist with the Treasury's cash management and investment activities.

Member Banks

Approximately 38 percent of the 8,039 commercial banks in the United States are members of the Federal Reserve System. National banks must be members; state-chartered banks may join if they meet certain requirements. The member banks are stockholders of the Reserve Bank in their District and as such, are required to hold 3 percent of their capital as stock in their Reserve Banks. Banks cannot sell or trade their Fed stock.

Other Depository Institutions

In addition to the approximately 3,000 member banks, about 17,000 other depository institutions provide checkable deposits and other banking services. These depository institutions include nonmember commercial banks, savings banks, savings and loan associations, and credit unions. Although not formally part of the Federal Reserve System, these institutions are subject to System regulations, including reserve requirements, and they have access to System payments services.

Activities

Banking Supervision & Regulation

The Federal Reserve System supervises and regulates a wide range of financial institutions and activities. The Federal Reserve works with other agencies to ensure that financial institutions safely manage their operations and provide fair and equitable services to consumers. Bank supervision involves monitoring and examining the condition of banks and their compliance with laws and regulations.

Several federal and state authorities regulate banks along with the Federal Reserve. The Office of the Comptroller of the Currency (OCC), the Federal Deposit Insurance Corporation (FDIC), the Office of Thrift Supervision (OTS) and the banking departments of various states also regulate financial institutions. The OCC charters regulates and supervises nationally chartered banks. The FDIC, the Federal Reserve and state banking authorities regulate state-chartered banks. Bank holding companies and financial services holding companies, which own or have controlling interest in one or more banks, are also regulated by the Federal Reserve. The OTS examines federal and many state-chartered thrift institutions, which include savings banks and savings and loan associations.

Consumer Protection

The Federal Reserve System administers consumer protection laws related to the banking system. Banks are required to provide customers clear and accurate information about services - such as savings accounts, loans and credit cards – and related requirements, rates, and fees. A bank's brochure for a savings account, for example, should include information on any minimum balance required, monthly service fee and the average percentage yield. In addition, the Truth in Lending Act requires banks to disclose the finance charge and the annual percentage rate so that a consumer can compare the prices of credit from different sources. It also limits liability on lost or stolen credit cards. These laws ensure that consumers and banks make decisions based on the same information.

Community Reinvestment

In accordance with the Community Reinvestment Act, the Federal Reserve reviews a bank's attempt to meet the credit and development needs of its entire community, sometimes including its efforts to lend in including low- and moderate- income areas. When deciding whether to approve an application for a bank acquisition or merger or for the formation of a bank holding company, the Federal Reserve takes into account an institution's performance under the CRA.

Regulations

The Board of Governors of the Federal Reserve System promulgated 18 distinct rules in the study period. Six of these were joint rules with other regulatory agencies. Of these rules:

- Seven (the majority related to the Truth in Lending Act) had disclosure or notification as the principal element, although some of these involved some degree of change in the practice that was disclosed;[292]
- Two expanded activities that qualified for Community Reinvestment Act consideration;[293]
- Two were essentially accounting matters;[294] and
- The other seven dealt with diverse topics, including:
  - Restrictions on credit card penalties and fees,[295]
  - Registration of mortgage originators under the S.A.F.E. Act,[296]
  - Modification of capital guidelines and risk-weight requirements to encourage participation in HUD's Making Home Affordable Program,[297]
  - Extensions for compliance dates with respect to another rule,[298]
  - Establishment of term accounts in the Federal Reserve System,[299]
  - SEC registration for credit rating agencies,[300] and
  - Internal agency procedures related to information requests under the Privacy Act.[301]

These rules can also be classified by the circumstances or objectives surrounding their promulgation:

- Ten rules[302] were promulgated specifically to implement requirements of the provisions of a recent statute;
- One rule[303] restricted practices but did not have a recent statute as the proximate cause;
- Three rules[304] expanded options of financial institutions (and were not mandatory), with the objective of benefitting distressed parts of the economy;

- Two rules[305] expanded options for financial institutions within the banking system;
- One rule[306] potentially expanded options for credit rating agencies; and
- One rule[307] was a simple housekeeping matter.

Federal Reserve regulations are somewhat unusual among independent regulatory agencies in that their scope can be much broader than the population that the agency directly regulates or supervises. Many Federal Reserve regulations apply to all depository institutions, not just to banks that are members of the Federal Reserve System. Some – particularly the Truth in Lending rules related to credit – apply to non-depository financial institutions (e.g., mortgage brokers) and to wide segments of the economy that happen to provide credit, such as retail trade, services, and utilities.

Analysis

Regulatory Flexibility Analysis

Exemption
The Board of Governors identified two rules as being exempt from RFA requirements.

- One rule had not had a NPRM and, if anything, benefitted the affected institutions;[308] and
- One rule, which adjusted reserve requirements, was exempt from the RFA definition of "rule."

Certification
The Board certified that five rules would not have a significant impact on a substantial number of small entities:

- One rule applied to internal agency procedures, not to business;
- One rule was elective and did not require the computational procedure that it allowed;
- One rule "does not require a financial institution to engage in these [CRA] activities;"

- One rule allowed several "potentially less burdensome alternatives" for compliance but did not address costs in the regulatory flexibility analysis;[309] and
- In one rule (S.A.F.E. Act) cited alternatives that had been adopted but did not explicitly discuss costs.

In one rule, the Board stated no conclusion about impacts, although this rule (the other CRA rule) clearly qualified for certification.

Certification is a checkpoint in regulatory flexibility analysis. If an agency can make this certification, the analysis ends; if the agency cannot make the certification, the analysis moves on to a new level of detail. The Board did not follow this pattern. Of the five rules certified (above), for example, the last two reported a FRFA.

In six other rules, the Board went through steps of a regulatory flexibility analysis after having stated a belief (4 rules) or an expectation (2 rules) that there would not be a significant impact on a substantial number of small entities. In the two "expect" instances, the Board referenced an IRFA and a request for comments. In three cases the basis for the belief (and certification) was clearly stated at the outset and was known in advance (two rules applied very narrowly, and one offered an extension of an exemption). Four of the analyses provided no additional findings to support a conclusion of no significant impacts on a substantial number of small entities,[310] and in one case an assumption about zero costs played a role in the findings. Only two rules drew comments (neither one that had mentioned requests for comments). None of these analyses discussed regulatory flexibility alternatives. These discussions were strikingly uninformative, and the analysis often was haphazard. These rules presented a pattern of weak analyses, most of which did no more than a certification with a short crisp explanatory paragraph would have done.

Need and Objectives

Discussion under this heading often began with the general objectives of the statute. Often the discussion really went no farther.[311] Sometimes the Board also cited statutory authority and/or summarized provisions of the rule. There were some clear statements of objective,[312] but these were generally on rules that were not directly implementing statutes. While about half of the rules were explicitly made to implement specific provisions of statutes, it was generally not clear whether and how the regulation went beyond the actual requirements of the statute. There was no sense of how much leeway for regulatory alternatives there might be.

Issues in Comments

The Board generally interpreted "comments" narrowly for purposes of regulatory flexibility analysis. For example: "The Board received no comments specifically addressing the initial regulatory flexibility analysis." As in that instance, the Board often reported receiving no comments. The lack of comments was often cited in support of the finding of no significant impacts on small businesses. The Board also cited the lack of information or data submitted in comments as a reason for not going into greater depth in its analysis. In a some cases, the Board accepted commenter's suggestion. In several cases where comments had contained objections, the Board (without going into detail) responded that the provisions to which the commenters objected were required by statute.

There was only one rule where the Board responded to comments in detail. In that case, SBA Advocacy submitted comments. The Board's responses are discussed further below.

Small Entities

The Board consistently made estimates of the number of small entities affected. Often this included detail such as the number of financial institutions in classes that might be affected by the rule; the total number and the number of small entities in a class; and the number of small entities affected by the rule.[313]

Where possible, the Board made use of available data, such as the number of banks it supervised or the number of entities filing a particular report. In some cases, an estimate from another rulemaking was cited. In some cases various sources were used, and the estimates were described as "tentative." In two cases, the percentage of small entities affected was estimated by a rough percentage estimate. In some regulations, (e.g., a rule affecting any business that might issue a gift card), the Board faced a herculean task, and it produced an estimate that was so broad that it was almost meaninglessly.[314]

While the estimates were nominally precise, the Board showed a limited inclination to refine their accuracy. In one rule, the IRFA contained two estimates of the number of mortgage brokers – 17,041 (Census data) and 53,000 (National Association of Mortgage Brokers estimate) – as well as the Board's own estimate,[315] and simply published them all with no attempt at reconciliation. In this case, the Board noted "the SBA also commented that the

Board failed to provide sufficient information about the number of small mortgage brokers that may be impacted by the rule." The Board responded that the RFA required it to provide "*where feasible*, an estimate of the number of small entities to which the proposed rule will apply" (emphasis in the original).

In a sense, the accuracy of the estimates was not very important. When tens of thousands of small entities are affected, there is no question about the "substantial number" prong of the certification test or that the impacts of the rule are widespread. The key question then becomes the size of impact on an individual small entity. Where impacts were not easily identifiable as small, the analyses were weak in this area, as there was rarely any quantitative analysis.

Reporting, Recordkeeping, and Other Compliance Requirements

A number of the rules had no compliance requirements – either inherently or because they were elective[316] – and some conferred positive benefits. The Board identified this sort of situation. In one case, the Board noted that the rule really did not apply to small businesses.[317]

In other cases, the Board identified the type of requirements (reporting, recordkeeping, or other). In one rule, the Board's discussion delimited the burden to "providing the disclosure itself." In most instances, the discussion generally recapitulated the provisions of the rule (among other topics) and provided general descriptions of such activities, but gave only a general operational description of compliance activities and their scope and did not estimate costs.

> Some small entities will be required, among other things, to alter certain business practices, develop new business models, re-train staff, and reprogram operational systems to ensure compliance [but] the effect of the final rule on small entities is unknown. The final rule could affect how loan originators are compensated and will impose certain related recordkeeping requirements on creditors. The precise costs that the final rule will impose on mortgage creditors and loan originators are difficult to ascertain.

The board compounded this lack of clarity in requirements by its inability to provide an estimate of baseline practices. The following (which appeared *verbatim* in preambles to two rules) is illustrative:

The Board notes that the precise costs to small entities to conform their open-end credit disclosures to the final rule and the costs of updating their systems to comply with the rule are difficult to predict. These costs depend on a number of factors that are unknown to the Board, including, among other things, the specifications of the current systems used by such entities to prepare and provide disclosures and administer credit card accounts, the complexity of the terms of the credit card products that they offer, and the range of such product offerings.

While such variability is common, this is the sort of situation where some type of sensitivity analysis using representative entities would be useful in assessing the significance of impacts, and there was none.

In one rule, SBA Advocacy commented the Board had not adequately assessed impacts of the proposed rule or proved that there was insufficient information about the impact for public comment. The Board stated:

The RFA... requires the IRFA to contain certain information including a description of the projected reporting, recordkeeping and other compliance requirements of the proposed rule, including an estimate of the classes of small entities which will be subject to the requirement and the type of professional skills necessary for preparation of the report or record... The RFA does not require that the Board be able to project the specific dollar amount that a rule will cost small entities in order to implement the rule; rather it requires a description of the projected impact of the rule on small entities and of reporting, recordkeeping, or compliance requirements... Accordingly, the Board described the projected impact of the proposed rule and sought comments from small entities themselves on the effect the proposed rule would have on their activities. First, the Board described the impact of the proposed rule on small entities by describing the rule's proposed requirements in detail throughout the supplementary information for the proposed rule. Second, the Board described the projected compliance requirements of the rule in its IRFA, noting the need for small entities to comply with recordkeeping requirements, and update systems and loan origination practices.[318]

Most of the Board's FRFAs contained no more information about impacts than this. The Board provided an actual cost estimate for only one rule.

Partial cost estimates were sometimes available in the Paperwork Reduction Act analysis, where the Board tended to base its estimates on the number of small banks it supervised. Two factors, however, substantially limited the usefulness of the PRA estimates.

- **Rounding.** When 40 person-hours appears in several diverse rules as the estimate for revision of policies and documents and related training – as well as twice in the same rule for activities under different sections – the estimate's accuracy seems questionable.
- **Averaging.** Averages for all sizes of entity and are useless for assessment on impacts on small entities. [319] Disproportionate impacts on small entities usually occur because diseconomies of small scale heighten impacts on very small businesses and/or some small businesses have to undertake more (or more costly) compliance activities.[320] Averaging obscures these differences in impacts,

Developing cost estimates has a variety of analytical benefits. The process helps an agency think through the impacts of the rule, including which small entities may be most seriously affected. Cost estimates are quite helpful in conveying the scope of the rule. Where costs are nontrivial, estimating them to some extent is an important tool for determining whether the economic impact will be significant. When a large number of entities are affected, an understanding of costs is critical for certification. The lack of cost information may be one reason that the Board only stated a belief about significant impacts in a majority of the rules.

Cost estimates also serve as grist for discussion. The Board stated repeatedly that there were no comments about the regulatory flexibility analysis. When one looks at the treatment of costs in these IRFAs (or FRFAs), however, there really is not a lot to comment about – except the lack of substance to comment about.

Minimization of Economic Impact on Small Entities

The Board believed or concluded that four of the rules (three of them truth-in-lending disclosure rules) would have a significant impact on a substantial number of small entities. Three of these rules incorporated explicit measures to minimize burdens:

- In two rules the Board developed (and in one case subsequently simplified) optional model forms "which can be used to ease compliance with the final rule."
- In one rule, the Board extended the rule's effective date for 100 days after the underlying Act went into effect.

- In one rule, the Board permitted institutions to rely on merchant, other institution, or other third party's coding of a transaction as a one-time or recurring debit card transaction.
- In one rule, the Board adopted (as commenters suggested) an alternative that permitted loan originator compensation to be based on loan amount.

In the fourth rule, the Board offered vague generalities:

> The Board sought to avoid imposing additional burden, while effectuating the statute in a manner that is beneficial to consumers... The Board did not receive any comment on any significant alternatives, consistent with the Credit Card Act, which would minimize impact of the final rule on small entities.

The S.A.F.E. Act

The S.A.F.E. Act rule provided the most quantitative analysis. Ironically, this was one of the rules that the Board certified as not having a significant impact on a substantial number of small entities.

The S.A.F.E. Act rule was a joint effort by six agencies. The rule required persons who act as a residential mortgage loan originators to be registered and required institutions that employ them to develop a policy and provide supervision. A *de minimis* provision provided a partial exemption from registration for certain employees,[321] and thus a substantial reduction in burden for their employers. Since the *de minimis* provision was only a partial exemption, institutions that originate mortgages still incurred compliance costs, but they were lower than costs of mortgage originators that did not qualify. Because of the structure of the partial exemption, the institutions that qualified tended to be among the smallest.

The Board produced an estimate of the number of small state member banks[322] affected (433) and an aggregate dollar estimate of compliance cost ($7.6 million). A thorough analysis would differentiate between small entities that were subject to *de minimis* requirements and those that were subject to full requirements and between initial (first-year) and ongoing (out-year) costs. The Board made neither distinction.[323] On a per-entity basis, the Board's estimate was comparable to the aggregate estimates of the OCC and OTS, and at the lower end for estimates of costs of entities subject to full regulation.[324]

The OCC and FDIC concluded that the costs of full compliance were not significant; the OTS concluded that they were significant.[325] In supporting its conclusion that costs were not significant, the Board stated that the aggregate cost was less than one percent of aggregate revenues of the affected banks. The aggregate cost that the Board reported ($7.6 million), however, was actually 3.2 percent of the aggregate revenue that the Board reported ($2.4 billion). For full-requirement banks, it appears that these costs were significant.

During the rulemaking, as a result of the comments and the subsequent analysis, the agencies made a number of modifications to address the economic impact on small entities:

- A second requirement for a *de minimis* exception – a threshold of mortgage loans originated for the institution – was removed;
- Detailed requirements for the written policies and procedures were trimmed;
- The amount of information required from a mortgage loan originator was reduced; and
- Loan modification actions and loss mitigation efforts were explicitly excluded from the definition of loan origination.

Assessment

The Board's regulatory flexibility analysis was often too incomplete to support any conclusion that was not fairly obvious. In most instances, where impacts probably were not significant, the effect may have been no worse than inefficiency. The Board followed the standard RFA format but at times appeared to be doing little more than going through the motions.

The Board was consistent in developing estimates of small entities and those that were affected by a regulation. The number of affected small entities usually was large. Corresponding estimates of impacts were usually lacking however, although types of compliance activities were usually well identified. Where quantitative estimates (including PRA) were made, they tended to be rough and lack detail.

The Board seemed reasonably responsive to public comments, sometimes incorporating them into rule modifications, although there seemed to be a lack of analytical initiative in the absence of public comments. Comments by SBA advocacy were another matter; the Board seemed largely to shrug them off. The rulemakings contained a number of modifications and alternatives, which clearly reflect a degree of awareness and concern about regulatory burdens.

The picture is somewhat blurred by the number of rules that were made jointly. In such circumstances, for example, it is not really possible to identify the initiative for regulatory flexibility alternatives. At least one rule provides a basis for comparison, however, and here the Board's analysis was less complete than that of either executive branch an one other independent agency that were involved.

12. Federal Trade Commission

Overview

The Federal Trade Commission (FTC)[326] is an independent agency, established in 1914 by the Federal Trade Commission Act. The FTC's mission includes both anti-trust activities and consumer protection. Over the years, Congress has directed the FTC to administer a wide variety of other consumer protection laws and has expanded its regulatory authority. The bureaus that make up the Commission reflect its mission.

Bureau of Consumer Protection

The Bureau of Consumer Protection works to protect consumers against unfair, deceptive, or fraudulent practices in the marketplace. The Bureau conducts investigations, sues companies and people who violate the law, develops rules to protect consumers, and educates consumers and businesses about their rights and responsibilities. The Bureau's seven divisions reflect the diversity of the FTC's consumer protection activities:

- **Advertising Practices** protects consumers by enforcing the nation's truth-in advertising laws.
- **Consumer and Business Education** plans, develops, and implements national campaigns to alert consumers to their rights and to explain compliance to industry.
- **Enforcement** litigates civil contempt and civil penalty actions to enforce FTC federal court injunctions and administrative orders that address consumer protection issues.
- **Financial Practices** protects consumers from deceptive and unfair practices in the financial services industry.
- **Marketing Practices** leads the Commission's response fraud and related practices that utilize the mails, the Internet, and other telecommunications.
- **Planning & Information** collects and analyzes complaints about consumer fraud and identity theft and makes them available to law enforcement agencies.

- **Privacy and Identity Protection** safeguards consumers' financial privacy.

Bureau of Competition

The FTC's Bureau of Competition promotes and protects free and vigorous competition by:

- Reviewing mergers and acquisitions, and challenging those that would likely lead to higher prices, fewer choices, or less innovation;
- Seeking out and challenging anticompetitive conduct in the marketplace, including monopolization and agreements between competitors;
- Promoting competition in industries where consumer impact is high, such as health care, real estate, oil & gas, technology, and consumer goods; and
- Providing information, and holding conferences and workshops, for consumers, businesses, and policy makers on competition issues and market analysis.

Bureau of Economics

The Bureau of Economics provides economic analysis and support to antitrust and consumer protection investigations and rulemakings. The Bureau also analyzes the economic impact of government regulation, and makes policy recommendations relating to competition and consumer protection.

Regulations

The FTC published 10 final rules that were included in the Unified Agenda in the study period.[327] One final rule was issued jointly with other financial regulatory agencies. Of these rules:

- Five rules (including one rescission) dealt with labeling or similar information requirements;[328]
- Four rules imposed or amended disclosure requirements and covered related business practices to some extent;[329] and
- One created a new optional form (jointly with other agencies).[330]

Analysis

Regulatory Flexibility Analysis

Exemption
Two of these final rules were treated as exempt from requirements of the RFA.

- One rule (a rescission) was exempt because it was published directly without a NPRM and public comment.
- One rule was issued as the result of a periodic review and did not entail any change to the existing regulation.

Certification
The FTC also certified that there was not a significant economic impact on a substantial number of small entities in half of the rulemakings.

- One rule provided an alternative, non-mandatory method of rating automotive fuel.
- Most depository institutions, the FTC opined in one instance, were already in compliance with the disclosure requirements of a new statute being implemented.
- In two labeling rules, the FTC included a FRFA "to explain the impacts of the amendments on small entities."

As these last two rules illustrate, the FTC tended to make a certification and then present a FRFA anyway. In two rules, the FTC was unable precisely to identify or to count the small entities, so that the "substantial number" could not be pinned down. In some instances the FTC said that the FRFA was done "to ensure that no such impact, if any, has been overlooked."

Need and Objectives
The FTC generally cited the statute, with the force of the statute ranging from an authorization to a mandatory requirements. Most of the rules seemed to be pretty direct implementations of statutory provisions. In most cases, the FTC also included a brief statement of purpose, such as:

> The objective of the proposed rule is to curb deceptive and unfair practices occurring in the MARS [mortgage assistance relief services]

industry... [It] is based on evidence in the record that deceptive and unfair acts are common in the provision of MARS to consumers.

Issues Raised by Commenters

In three of these regulations, the FTC reported that it had received no comments about the impacts on small businesses. In two cases, the FTC cited statutory requirements to demonstrate that it could not accommodate the comment. Overall, however, the FTC seemed fairly responsive to comments and often made some type of adjustment in response. In some rules, cost estimates were increased considerably in response to comments. Two other examples:

- In a disclosure rule, commenters expressed concern about the proposed requirement of a separate internet "landing page." The FTC changed the requirement to including the disclosure on every web page where this particular offer was announced.
- In a regulation covering the mortgage assistance relief services (MARS) industry, the FTC had proposed a ban on advance fees. There was considerable concern about the impact on small entities, particularly attorneys. The FTC noted that "several small firms and sole practitioners owned by attorneys asserted that they would go out of business if the Commission imposed an advance fee ban." The FTC responded by providing an exemption from recordkeeping and compliance requirements for small attorney providers who meet certain conditions, and by allowing them to receive payments from a client trust account (a mechanism for avoiding the advanced fee ban) – in effect an alternative standard.

Small Entities to Which the Rule Applies

In two instances (both related to consumer finance) the FTC was unable to identify small entities, for lack of data, adding in one case:

the entities under the Commission's jurisdiction are so varied that there is no way to identify them in general and, therefore, no way to know how many of them qualify as small businesses.

In the other rules, the FTC gave concise descriptions of the entities covered. Estimates of the numbers varied from quite precise (one rule), a rough round number (three rules), to really not thinking there were any (one rule). In two instances, the FTC cited data from past warnings or enforcement actions of analogous rules in estimating the numbers of entities affected.

For two of the reporting rules involving product labeling, the affected population was divided into manufacturers and catalogue retailers. Most (in one case, probably all) of the small businesses were retailers, and costs for them were relatively minor.

Projected Reporting, Recordkeeping, and Other Compliance Requirements

The FTC was generally clear in describing the outlines, and in some cases the details, of the requirements. In some instances cost estimates were available from the Paperwork Reduction Act analyses. Although these were not representative of small businesses, they were clear, logically constructed, and fairly detailed.[331] In several instances the general size of a cost was indicated, and estimated costs usually were minimal. These discussions, while not precise, were generally adequate to support the proposition that costs were not particularly significant.

Steps taken to Minimize Significant Impact on Small Businesses

The FTC fairly consistently identified some measures. There was one exception[332]:

> The amendments closely track the prescriptive requirements of the statute, and thus leave little room for significant alternatives to decrease the burden on regulated entities.

Some labeling requirements specified the format. Other disclosure and other information requirements, however, were usually performance standards – what information to provide, not how. In two instances the use of forms was optional, not mandatory.

The FTC also took a number of specific steps to make rules less burdensome. The general techniques included:

- Use of delayed (and thoughtfully timed) effective dates – extended in one rule;
- Substitution of less burdensome provisions;
- Provision of multiple options for compliance, including optional model forms;[333]
- Limiting specific provisions to entities to which they were most relevant;

- A conditional, but fairly extensive, exemption (the MARS rule described above).

The FTC was unwilling to adopt an across-the-board exemption for small entities. The reasoning was similar to that of financial regulation agencies:

> The protections afforded to consumers are equally important regardless of the size of the MARS provider with whom they transact. Indeed, small MARS providers have no unique attributes that would warrant exempting them from provisions, such as the required disclosures or conduct prohibitions. The information provided in the disclosures is material to the consumer regardless of the size of the entity offering the services.

Assessment

The FTC has been fairly consistent in the use of regulatory flexibility concepts and techniques. Certifications of no significant impact on substantial numbers of small entities are well supported in cases where they are not obvious. Affected entities were clearly identified and enumerated where practical. Compliance activities were usually adequately described. Estimates of cost from (from related analyses) are sometimes broken down on a per-entity basis and by type of cost instead of just aggregates, which is particularly useful when the number of entities affected is not clear. The FTC seemed generally responsive to comments, in adjusting cost estimates as well as in making modifications to reduce burdens. Alternatives to provide options or otherwise reduce burdens were often incorporated. Overall, the FTC's performance was relatively solid.

13. National Credit Union Administration

Overview

The National Credit Union Administration (NCUA)[334] is the independent federal agency that charters and supervises federal credit unions. The Federal Credit Union Act (1934) – designed to make credit available and promote thrift through a national system of nonprofit, cooperative credit unions - authorized the formation of federally chartered credit unions in all states. The Bureau of Federal Credit Unions originally was housed at the Farm Credit Administration. Regulatory responsibility shifted over the years as the agency moved from the Federal Deposit Insurance Corporation to the Federal Security Agency, and then the Department of Health, Education and Welfare.

In 1970, the National Credit Union Administration was reconstituted as an independent agency, and the National Credit Union Share Insurance Fund (NCUSIF) was formed to insure credit union deposits. In 1977, legislation expanded services available to credit union members, including share certificates and mortgage lending. In 1979, Congress created the Central Liquidity Facility, the credit union lender of last resort. In 1985, Congress authorized recapitalization of the NCUSIF. Federally insured credit unions deposited 1 percent of their shares into the Share Insurance Fund, and since then the NCUA Board has only charged credit unions a premium when the Fund dropped to a 1.25 percent equity ratio. The NCUSIF is backed by the "full faith and credit of the United States Government."

Regulations
NCUA published 15 final rules that were included in the Unified Agenda in the study period.

- Three relaxed existing regulations in a way that allowed credit unions to participate in a Federal program or provide a new service (to the benefit of the credit unions);[335]
- Five made minor changes involving clarifications, definitions, or other technical matters;[336]
- Two affected only corporate credit unions, which are virtually all large businesses;[337]
- Two were joint involving half a dozen agencies rules mandated by legislation, of which:
    - One was voluntary and had costs that were probably minor,[338] and
    - One had possibly significant costs on nearly 10 percent of small credit unions;[339]
- One pertained to procedures used only for mergers and conversions;[340]
- One withdrew the substance of a previous rule;[341] and
- One rescinded four "RegFlex" exemptions for well-performing credit unions.[342]

Most of these rules appeared to have little or no adverse impact on small credit unions. The rule with the greatest impacts applied only to large credit unions – which seems fitting, as recent financial turmoil has been due to practices of large financial institutions. At least two others clearly did have adverse impacts.

Analysis

Small Entities

The NCUA uses a size threshold of $10 million in assets. By contrast, the SBA standard for depository financial institutions,[343] which is used by other financial regulatory agencies, is $175 million in assets. Credit Unions are generally much smaller than banks and savings institutions. The NCUA estimated that just over half (3,056 of 7,710) of the credit unions[344] that it regulates are small by this definition.[345]

Regulatory Flexibility Analysis

Certification

Thirteen rules were – or could have been - certified[346] by the NCUA as not having a significant economic impact on a substantial number of small entities. Eight of these certifications were based on a brief – often one-sentence - explanation, which generally did appear reasonable.

- Three rules were certified because they imposed no burden and gave credit unions added flexibility;
- Two rules were certified because they applied only to corporate credit unions, only one of which fits NCUA's definition of small;
- Two rules were certified because the rule was only a clarification;[347] and
- One rule on mergers and conversions of credit unions was certified because very few credit unions merge or convert in any given year.[348]

In two other instances no basis was given for the certification, although any impacts of the rule were pretty clearly minor.

- One rule revised two definitions, defined a third term, and clarified some existing requirements; and
- One rule amended regulations and staff interpretations to conform to other rules, including a Federal Reserve regulation.

In two instances, the NCUA did not even make a certification, although it was fairly clear that a certification would have been justified.

- One rule simply withdrew a former rule; and
- One rule required a change in signage to reflect a statutory increase in the standard maximum share insurance.

In one rule, the NCUA rescinded four exemptions that had been granted to federal credit unions that qualified for a RegFlex program by virtue of being demonstrably well capitalized. In lieu of a regulatory flexibility analysis, the NCUA stated:

> This rule enhances safety and soundness without additional regulatory burden. Accordingly, this will not have a significant economic impact on a substantial number of small credit unions, and therefore, no regulatory flexibility analysis is required.

A majority of commenters objected to two of the rescissions, pointing out clear business advantages of the exemption. The NCUA did not make any attempt to describe or estimate impacts of loss of these exemptions, although a sort of phase-in was incorporated. An NCUA representative explained that small credit unions are too small to engage in the sort of practices where the exemptions would have created a business advantage. Thus only large credit unions were actually affected. The analysis should have included this explanation and some estimates of the number of small credit unions (if any) that participated in the RegFlex Program.

Analysis
Two of the rules were promulgated jointly with several other federal agencies.

- Development of a standard form for privacy notices under the Gramm-Leach-Bliley Act ("GLB Act"); and
- Registration and procedural requirements under the S.A.F.E. Mortgage Licensing Act.

Both rulemakings included relatively extensive regulatory flexibility analyses, but regulatory flexibility issues were addressed in differing degrees by different agencies. Because of the joint authorship, it is not possible to tell what NCUA's role may have been in devising regulatory flexibility alternatives.

In the GLB Act regulation, the NCUA was one of the least visible of all agencies. Under the heading "Small Entities Subject to the Rules," the NCUA "estimate[d] that 3,168 federally-insured, state-chartered credit unions are small entities for purposes of the RFA." The NCUA appears only one other time in the text of the notice.[349] The consensus conclusion of the agencies was that there would not be significant impacts on small entities because use of the form was not mandatory.

The S.A.F.E. Mortgage Licensing Act regulation required registration of financial institution employees who act as a residential mortgage loan originators and oversight of their employees. There was a *de minimis* exception for employees,[350] and (by extension) for credit unions, although credit unions with no registered employees still incurred some monitoring and procedural costs. The NCUA did a detailed analysis of how many small credit unions would be subject to the rule and how many of those would qualify for a de minimis exemption. The analysis concluded that 1,073 small credit unions (25.8 percent of all small credit unions) would be subject to the regulation because the originated loans, and 280 small credit unions (9.2 percent) would be subject to the full impact of the rule. Without making cost estimates, NCUA then cited the "above reasons" as the basis for certification that there would not be a significant impact on a substantial number of small credit unions. Other agencies (prodded by SBA to improve their analysis) estimated that the costs for small banks and savings institutions subject to the full rule would be $17,000 to $25,000, although the agencies differed in their conclusions about the significance of these costs.

Regulatory Flexibility Alternatives

Whatever its role in the joint regulations, the NCUA did devise a creative accommodation in its rule rescinding the RegFlex exemptions.[351] Credit unions that were actively using exemptions were grandfathered at their current levels, but in a way that could only ratchet downwards (with no fixed deadline). Thus, for example, if a credit union exceeded the limit on fixed assets, its level of fixed assets could fall toward the limit but never increase. The NCUA also promised to make a waiver process more accessible.

Assessment

The NCUA did little or no real regulatory flexibility analysis. In most cases, impacts seem minor enough that the NCUA probably reached a reasonable conclusion of no significant impacts on a substantial number of small entities. Presentation was formulaic and minimalist, usually consisting of a single paragraph stating the certification and basis, and sometimes not even that. The NCUA showed itself capable of estimating the number of small credit unions affected by a regulation with reasonable precision but did not do that consistently. None of the write-ups reflected any attempt to describe or assess impacts on credit unions, even in response to comments. At best, the analysis was rudimentary and incomplete.

14. National Indian Gaming Commission

Overview

The National Indian Gaming Commission (NIGC)[352] was established as an independent federal regulatory agency pursuant to the Indian Gaming Regulatory Act of 1988 (Act). The NIGC has the general duty to "promulgate such regulations and guidelines as it deems appropriate to implement the provisions of" the Act. The Commission's primary mission is to

- Regulate gaming activities on Indian lands for the purpose of shielding Indian tribes from organized crime and other corrupting influences;
- Ensure that Indian tribes are the primary beneficiaries of gaming revenue; and
- Assure that gaming is conducted fairly and honestly by both operators and players.

To achieve these goals, the Commission is authorized to

- Conduct investigations;
- Undertake enforcement actions, including the issuance of violation, assessment of civil fines, and/or issuance of closure orders;
- Conduct background investigations;
- Conduct audits; and
- Review and approve Tribal gaming ordinances.

The NIGC's regulations are codified in Title 25 of the Code of Federal Regulations, Part 501 to 599.

Regulations

All of the NIGC "Completed Actions" listed in the Spring 2010, Fall 2010, or Spring 2011 Unified Agenda were withdrawals of reviews, previous Interim Rules or NPRMs. Thus no further analysis was done on NIGC regulations.

15. National Labor Relations Board

Overview

The National Labor Relations Board (NLRB)[353] is an independent federal agency vested with the power to safeguard employees' rights to organize and to determine whether to have unions as their bargaining representative. The agency also acts to prevent and remedy unfair labor practices committed by private sector employers and unions. The NLRB:

- **Conducts elections** to determine whether a majority of employees want to form or join a union, or to decertify an existing union;
- **Investigates charges** alleging unfair labor practices under Section 8 of the National Labor Relations Act;
- **Facilitates settlements of meritorious charges of unfair labor practices to avoid** litigation whenever possible;
- **Decides cases on unfair labor practices through hearings before** Administrative Law Judges, with appeals heard by the Board;
- **Enforces orders** in the U.S. Courts of Appeals, as necessary.

The National Labor Relations Board's regulations are codified in Title 29 of the Code of Federal Regulations, Part 100 to 199.

Regulations

The National Labor Relations Board had no regulations listed in the Spring 2010, Fall 2010, or Spring 2011 Unified Agenda as "Final Rule Stage" or "Completed Action." Thus no further analysis was done on NLRB regulations.

16. Nuclear Regulatory Commission

Overview

The U.S. Nuclear Regulatory Commission (NRC)[354] was created as an independent agency by Congress in 1974, replacing the Atomic Energy Commission. The Commission's mission is to regulate the nation's civilian use of byproduct, source, and special nuclear materials to ensure adequate protection of public health and safety, to promote the common defense and security, and to protect the environment. NRC's regulatory mission covers three main areas:

- **Reactors**: Commercial reactors for generating electric power and research and test reactors used for research, testing, and training;
- **Waste**: Transportation, storage, and disposal of nuclear materials and waste, and decommissioning of nuclear facilities from service; and
- **Materials**: Uses of nuclear materials in medical, industrial, and academic settings and facilities that produce nuclear fuel.

Specific NRC regulatory objectives include:

- Provision of an ample margin of safety from radiation that was generated by the activities of its licensees;
- Prevention of a major reactor accident that would result in a massive release of radiation that could threaten public health and safety;
- Safe management of high-level and low-level radioactive waste; and
- Protection of nuclear materials from theft or diversion.

Regulations

NRC published 17 final rules that were included in the Unified Agenda in the study period. Of these rules:

- Five rules dealt with administrative matters or clarifications and were not subject to the APA notice and review process.[355]
- One rule reduced the range of circumstances requiring an Environmental Assessment.[356]
- Five rules concerned storage of spent nuclear fuel.[357]
- Three rules affected the operation of nuclear power plants.[358]
- Two rules concerned transportation of nuclear materials.[359]
- One rule set annual fees for NRC licensees.[360]

Analysis

Regulatory Flexibility Analysis

In all but one of the rulemakings, NRC certified that the rule would not have a significant economic impact on a substantial number of small entities. In most cases, this certification was straightforward:

- The five rules concerning NRC administrative changes were not subject to the notice and comment provisions of the Administrative Procedures Act rule. Thus they were exempt from the RFA.
- Neither nuclear power plants nor independent spent fuel storage installations are small business by either SBA size standards[361] or the size standards established by the NRC at 10 CFR 2.810."[362] Thus certification was virtually automatic for the eight rules that applied only to these entities.
- For one of the transportation-related rules, the NRC stated that, because of the companies regulated, "this rule... does not fall within the scope of the definition of 'small entities'." In the other it said only that "a majority of companies" are small. In both cases the rule changes were relatively small. They lacked any obvious significant adverse impacts and may on balance have been helpful.
- The rule on categorical exclusions from environmental review clearly eased regulatory requirements, although it was not entirely clear whether the chief beneficiary was private business or the NRC itself.[363]

One rule set annual fees for all NRC licensees.[364] The total amount of fees to be collected was tied to NRC's budget.[365] Based on recent data, NRC estimated that "about 26 percent of these licensees (approximately 1,000 licensees) qualified as small entities" – predominantly nuclear materials users. Based on comments and review of license termination data, NRC concluded that adverse impacts of a single fee could be substantial. After considering several fee structures, NRC selected a maximum fee for small entities. NRC subsequently added a second tier of very small entities,[366] with a much lower cap to the fee. Originally the annual fee caps for small entities and for small entities were set in dollar terms. Eventually NRC evolved a system in which:

- The small-entity maximum annual fee was set at 39 percent of the average for all fee categories for the previous two years; and

- The very-small-entity maximum annual fee was set as 22 percent of the small-entity maximum (8.6 percent of the overall two-year fee average).

Assessment

Nuclear reactors and nuclear waste handlers regulated by the NRC are virtually all large entities. Thus, even when a regulation is not exempt from the RFA, little analysis is really needed by the NRC. The picture changes for materials users, many of which are small. In the one rule reviewed where this was an issue, the MNRC executed the basic elements of a regulatory flexibility analysis and developed a classic regulatory flexibility alternative – a tiered fee schedule – to fit the situation.

17. Occupational Safety and Health Review Commission

Overview

The Occupational Safety and Health Review Commission (OSHRC)[367] is an independent federal agency that provides administrative trial and appellate review under the Occupational Safety and Health Act of 1970. The OSHRC was created to decide contests of citations or penalties under the OSH Act resulting from Occupational Safety and Health Administration (OSHA) inspections of American work places. The Review Commission functions as a two-tiered administrative court, with established procedures for:

- Conducting hearings, receiving evidence and rendering decisions by its Administrative Law Judges (ALJs); and
- Discretionary review of ALJ decisions by a panel of Commissioners.

Decisions of the three OSHRC Commissioners may be appealed to an appropriate United States Court of Appeals.

Regulations

The Occupational Safety and Health Administration's regulations are codified in Title 29 of the Code of Federal Regulations, Part 1900 to 1999. The OSHRC itself does not regulate industry or enforce the OSH Act. It is concerned solely with the adjudication of disputes under the OSH Act.

18. Postal Regulatory Commission

Overview

The Postal Regulatory Commission is an independent agency that has exercised regulatory oversight over the U. S. Postal Service (USPS) since its creation by the Postal Reorganization Act of 1970. The Postal Accountability and Enhancement Act (PAEA) enacted on December 20, 2006, significantly strengthened the Commission's authority to serve as a counterbalance to new flexibility granted to the Postal Service in setting postal rates.

The Act requires the Commission to develop and maintain regulations for a modern system of rate regulation, consult with the Postal Service on delivery service standards and performance measures, consult with the Department of State on international postal policies, prevent cross-subsidization or other anticompetitive postal practices, promote transparency and accountability, and adjudicate complaints. The law also assigns new and continuing oversight responsibilities to the PRC, including annual determinations of Postal Service compliance with applicable laws, development of accounting practices and procedures for the Postal Service, review of the Universal Service requirement, and assurance of transparency through periodic reports.[368]

Regulations

The PRC promulgated two regulations in 2010. Both pertain to reports by the USPS to the PRC concerning the quality of service. One regulation prescribed the content and form of the reports.[369] The other designated specific services that are exempted from reporting requirements.[370]

Analysis

The PRC's regulations apply only to the USPS. Accordingly, the PRC did not conduct any economic impact analysis or regulatory flexibility.

19. Recovery Accountability and Transparency Board

Overview

The Recovery Accountability and Transparency Board (RATB)[371] was created by the American Recovery and Reinvestment Act of 2009. Its mission is:

To promote accountability by coordinating and conducting oversight of Recovery funds to prevent fraud, waste, and abuse and to foster transparency on Recovery spending by providing the public with accurate, user-friendly information.

The Board has two principal goals:

- To provide transparency of Recovery-related funds and
- To detect and prevent fraud, waste, and mismanagement.

Regulations

The three regulations that RATB promulgated in the study period were essentially housekeeping rules related to the start-up status of the agency. These regulations pertained to public access to RATB records under the Privacy Act of 1974[372] and the Freedom of Information Act.[373] Most of the substance of these rules concerned internal RATB operations. They had impacts on the public only in the sense of setting requirements for access – providing identifying information and paying actual costs of access or duplication - which were minimal.

Analysis

To the extent that there were any effects outside the agency, these rules affected only the general public. Accordingly, the RATB did not perform economic impact or regulatory flexibility analysis.

20. Securities and Exchange Commission

Overview

The U.S. Securities and Exchange Commission (SEC)[374] is an independent federal agency, which holds primary responsibility for enforcing the federal securities laws and regulating the securities industry, the nation's stock and options exchanges, and other electronic securities markets in the United States, as well as participants in those markets, including securities brokers and dealers, investment advisors, and mutual funds. The mission of the SEC is to protect investors, maintain fair, orderly, and efficient markets, and facilitate capital formation.

The SEC's operating principle is that all investors, whether large institutions or private individuals, should have access to certain basic facts about an investment prior to buying it, and so long as they hold it. To achieve its mandate, the SEC requires public companies to submit quarterly and annual reports, as well as other periodic reports, which disclose meaningful financial and other information to the public. This provides a common pool of knowledge for all investors to use to judge for themselves whether to buy, sell, or hold a particular security. Disclosure of financial and other information about the issuer and the security itself also increases public scrutiny and helps reduce insider trading and fraud.

The SEC maintains an online database called EDGAR (the Electronic Data Gathering, Analysis, and Retrieval system), from which investors can access this and other information filed with the agency. The SEC also has the authority to bring civil enforcement actions against individuals or companies alleged to have committed accounting fraud, provided false information, or engaged in insider trading or other violations of the securities law.

The SEC is responsible for administering eight major laws that govern the securities industry:

- The Securities Act of 1933 has a dual objective:
  - Require that investors receive financial and other significant information concerning securities being offered for public sale; and
  - Prohibit deceit, misrepresentations, and other fraud in the sale of securities. Disclosure of important financial information through the registration of securities is a primary means of accomplishing these goals
- The Securities Exchange Act of 1934 created the Securities and Exchange Commission and gave it broad authority over the securities industry, including the power to:
  - Register, regulate, and oversee brokerage firms, transfer agents, clearing agencies, self-regulatory organizations (SROs),[375]
  - Discipline regulated entities that engage in conduct prohibited by the Act, and
  - Require periodic reporting of information by companies with publicly traded securities.
- **The Trust Indenture Act of 1939** sets standards that apply to debt securities such as bonds, debentures, and notes that are offered for public sale.
- **The Investment Company Act of 1940** regulates the organization of companies, including mutual funds, that engage primarily in

investing, reinvesting, and trading in securities, and whose own securities are offered to the investing public. The Act requires these companies to disclose their financial condition and investment policies to investors when stock is initially sold and, subsequently, on a regular basis.

- **The Investment Advisers Act of 1940** requires that firms or sole practitioners compensated for advising others about securities investments must register with the SEC and conform to regulations designed to protect investors.
- **The Sarbanes-Oxley Act of 2002** mandates a number of reforms to enhance corporate responsibility, enhance financial disclosures and combat corporate and accounting fraud.
- **The Credit Rating Agency Reform Act of 2006** requires nationally recognized statistical rating organizations (NRSROs) to register with the Securities and Exchange Commission (SEC) and otherwise sought to improve ratings quality for the protection of investors by fostering accountability, transparency, and competition in the credit rating agency industry.
- **The Dodd-Frank Wall Street Reform and Consumer Protection Act** has a variety of provisions designed to prevent another significant financial crisis by creating new financial regulatory processes that enforce transparency and accountability while implementing rules for consumer protection. The Dodd-Frank act is the basis for most recent SEC rulemakings.

Regulations

The SEC published 23 final sets of rules that were included in the Unified Agenda in the study period. Six of these rules were interim final rules, temporary rules, or extensions of interim final rules. One final rule was issued jointly with other financial regulatory agencies. Of these rules:

- Six concerned disclosure requirements, including:
  - Three setting disclosure requirements for securities,[376]
  - One setting disclosure requirements for shareholder proxy materials,[377] and
  - One requiring disclosures about nationally recognized statistical rating organizations;[378]
- Five concerned operations and practices of regulated entities (usually including records);[379]

- Four concerned requirements for reporting to or filing with the SEC;[380]
- Two concerned requirements for registering with the SEC;[381]
- Two primarily included requirements for shareholder votes (with some disclosure);[382]
- Three concerned some aspect of a form or notification, including:
  - Creation (with other agencies) of a standardized (optional) privacy notice form,[383]
  - Modification of information given on a form related to NRSROs,[384] and
  - Permitting proxy information to be provided over the internet;[385]
- One allowed a limited exemption to SEC rules for tactical purposes;[386] and
- One concerned only internal procedures.[387]

Analysis

Small Entities and the Regulated Population

The SEC has set – by regulation – its own definitions of small entities for purposes of the Regulatory Flexibility Act. These are quite different from the SBA size standard, which is $7 million in revenues for the relevant industries.[388] In addition to not being affiliated with or controlled by an entity that is not "small," SEC size thresholds, which are defined under different authorizing acts, include:

- An "issuer" or "person"[389] other than an investment company: $5 million in assets;[390]
- A broker or dealer: $500,000 in total capital;[391]
- A municipal securities dealer:
  - $10 million in total assets and
  - $100,000 per month in municipal securities transaction;[392]
- An exchange: Has been exempted from reporting requirements of Exchange Act Rule 601;[393]
- Investment company or group of investment companies: $50 million in net assets;[394]
- An investment advisor:
  - $5 million in total assets and
  - $25 million in assets under management;[395]
- A security clearing agency:

- $500 million in securities transactions and
- $200 million of funds and securities in its custody or control.[396]

The size distribution of the population of financial entities that the SEC regulates is different from that of the general business population, which is highly skewed. In absolute or relative terms – or both - few entities of most types registered with the SEC are small. SEC estimates[397] in these rulemakings included the following:

- Public companies (or issuers): 1,100 to 1,229 are small.
- Brokers and dealers: 890 to 915 (17 percent) are small.
- Investment Advisors: 680 to 781 (6 percent) are small.
- Business development companies: 31 to 33 are small.
- Sponsors of asset-backed securities: One small entity was identified.
- Nationally recognized statistical rating organizations: 2 (out of 30) are small.
- Non-SRO trading centers: 5 (out of 407) are small.
- SROs: None is small.

Many SEC rules apply to specific activities or types of transactions that typically are done by large entities. Because of their limited application, some of the rules affected only a fraction of the small entities of their type. One rule, for example, affected an estimated 21 broker-dealers. For investment advisors, three rules were estimated to affect 38, 61, and 73, respectively.

Regulatory Flexibility Analysis

Certification
The SEC made conservative use of the certification that there would not be a significant impact on a substantial number of small entities. Seven of the rules reviewed were certified. Of these:

- Two were extensions of an existing rule that had no impacts, and they presented an alternative compliance mechanism that was voluntary.
- Two affected a very small number of entities: Two NRSROs in both instances, plus a sponsor of asset-backed securities in one case.
- Two affected no small entities.
- No explanation was given in one case.

There were also two rules for which no regulatory flexibility analysis was done, but which were not formally certified.

- One affected only recipients of TARP funds.
- One affected only internal SEC procedures.

Need For and Objectives of Rule

The SEC generally provided reasonably concise summaries of the objectives of the rule. While many of these rules were required by statute (particularly the Dodd-Frank Act), the SEC avoided just giving a formulaic statement of that fact.

In a temporary rule promulgated to meet an imminent statutory deadline, for example, the SEC stated: "This rule and form are necessary so that municipal advisors can meet this Congressional mandate and continue to function as municipal advisors."

Significant Issues Raised in Public Comments

There were comments on most of the rules for which the SEC did a regulatory flexibility analysis. Many of these comments explicitly or implicitly suggested a complete or partial exemption for small businesses. Some did little more than state that small businesses would be burdened; some explained why. Some offered suggestions on how to modify the rule.

The SEC was generally responsive. Often the response was that the commenter was addressing something that was necessary to the regulation or required by law. (See discussion below about exemptions.) In some cases, the SEC explained something about the regulation that mitigated the impact the commenter was addressing. Where there was an operational suggestion, the SEC did appear to have considered it. In some cases it was rejected. In several cases, however, the SEC modified the rule to address the problem.

Small Entities Subject to the Rule

The SEC consistently identified types of entities that would be affected[398] and estimated the number actually affected – not just the number of small entities. This job was doubtless simplified by the fact that – in most cases – the effected entities were registered with the Commission, but the SEC made good use of these data.

Reporting, Recordkeeping, and Other Reporting Requirements

The nature of this discussion varied with the type of rule. In the majority of cases, the SEC provided a fairly clear recap of the information to be provided (disclosures), the forms to fill out and/or types of records to be kept, the procedures to be developed, and/or the actions to be taken. The information was specific but not detailed.

In several cases, there was virtually no reported impact. This included an extension of an existing rule and a rule changing information provided on a form, among others. In a few cases the discussion veered off into the number of small entities that would be affected and/or measures to minimize small business impacts.

Further detail was provided in Paperwork Reduction Act and Benefit-Cost analyses. In most cases it was difficult to cross-walk this information into the regulatory flexibility analysis because it was based on analysis of the affected entities as a whole (most of which were large), and because the analysis appeared to use a subset of the affected population for most specific costs. In a several cases, however, the numbers were small enough to confirm that small-business impacts would be small. In one of these cases the SEC segmented the paperwork analysis by three sizes of entity, using a standard for "small" that was much larger than the RFA standard.

Exemption

The SEC consistently declined to exempt small entities. This was one area in which it consistently rejected comments. In some instances, the discussion addressed specific implications of an exemption. In the end (and usually at the beginning) the SEC gave some variant of the argument that an exemption was incompatible with the law and/or the purposes of the regulation. At times, the SEC suggested that an exemption would violate equal protection under the laws. In one instance, for example, the SEC declined to exempt small entities, because:

> the purpose of the rules is to facilitate the exercise of shareholders' traditional State law rights [and] we believe that shareholders of smaller reporting companies should be able to exercise these rights to the same extent as shareholders of larger reporting companies.

Different Reporting or Compliance Requirements or Timetables

The SEC took a similar stance about differential compliance requirements as it did on exemptions – but not as reflexively or absolutely. For example:

We considered different compliance standards for the small entities that will be affected by the amendments [but] we are not aware of any different standards that would be consistent with the purposes of the amendments.

Having taken that default stance, the SEC then proceeded to make modifications in a number of cases that either were explicitly for small businesses or addressed concerns that had been raised with respect to small businesses:

- Regulation S-K allowed small businesses to file an abbreviated report on executive compensation. Two new rules added to disclosure requirements, but retained the previous allowance – thus in effect exempting them from some aspects of the new disclosure requirements.
- Another rule referred to an existing limited exception, which was retained, and added a new one.
- Two rules delayed the compliance date for small businesses by two years.[399]
- Another rule allowed a two-year phase-in for shareholder voting requirements.
- One rule, which was designed to curb "pay to play" practices, prohibited making payment to a third party for soliciting business from any government entity. A carefully crafted limited exception was provided for small businesses, who are relatively likely to contract out marketing activities.
- Use of the form developed in one rule was voluntary, and some provisions in two rules represented voluntary alternatives to existing procedures.

In some instances, the SEC had limited flexibility because the statutory requirements were quite specific. Nevertheless, the SEC appeared willing to make some exceptions for small businesses where it saw the need and could figure out how to do it consistent with objectives.

Clarification, Consolidation, or Simplification of Reporting and Compliance Requirements
The SEC made no measures of this type for small businesses. On the other hand, the SEC frequently asserted that it had made the requirements as simple

as possible for everyone. In several of the rules, clarification was an objective,[400] and providing clearer information for the investor was a general objective of many of them.

Performance Rather than Design Standards
    The SEC's position on performance standards varied. To the extent that the rule involved a specific form, the scope for performance standards was limited. In some rules, the SEC used design standards for reasons that were explained.[401] In many instances, however, the SEC stated that it was using performance standards, citing such things as the absence of specification of format or details of content of required notices. It seems clear that the SEC was aware of and considering performance standards.

Assessment
    The SEC consistently followed and reported in the standard format of a regulatory flexibility analysis – in substance as well as form. Development of an extensive and varied set of small business standards provided a solid foundation for analysis of small entities. Although quantitative impacts on small entities were not generally estimated, the nature and scope were fairly well delineated, and the entities affected were consistently identified and counted. Certifications of no significant impact on a substantial number of small entities were well documented. Given the tendency for SEC regulations to target large entities, the SEC seemed conservative in its use of certification. Discussions, explanations, and responses to comments were generally clear and reasonable. The SEC's use of regulatory flexibility alternatives is constrained by the specifics of the statutes and by its own sense of fiduciary responsibility, which (as with other financial regulatory agencies) construes exemption as inherently contrary to its mandate. Nevertheless, the SEC seemed generally aware of the issues, included regulatory flexibility alternatives in a number of cases, and showed itself capable (in the "pay to play") regulation of creativity in this area. Over all, the SEC's regulatory flexibility analysis is quite creditable.

21. Surface Transportation Board

Overview
    The Surface Transportation Board (STB) was created in the ICC Termination Act of 1995 and is the successor agency to the Interstate

Commerce Commission. The STB is an economic regulatory agency that Congress charged with resolving railroad rate and service disputes and reviewing proposed railroad mergers. The STB is independent in its decisions, although it is administratively affiliated with the Department of Transportation.

The STB serves as both an adjudicatory and a regulatory body. The agency has jurisdiction over railroad rate and service issues and rail restructuring transactions (mergers, line sales, line construction, and line abandonments); certain trucking company, moving van, and non-contiguous ocean shipping company rate matters; certain intercity passenger bus company structure, financial, and operational matters; and rates and services of certain pipelines not regulated by the Federal Energy Regulatory Commission. Within the STB:

- The Office of the General Counsel provides legal advice and defends STB actions in court;
- The Office of Economics gathers and reports data; performs economic and policy analysis in support of Board decisions and applied economic analysis, most notably the development of the STB's costing system; and audits Class I railroads;
- The Office of Environmental Analysis undertakes environmental reviews of actions; and
- The Office of the Managing Director handles agency administrative matters.

Regulations

During the study period, the STB promulgated two rules, both of which involved jurisdiction over rail carriers.

- One rule - adopted in response to legislation, which removed most STB jurisdiction over waste rail transfer facilities in favor of state regulation - established land-useexemption permits for siting as an alternative to state siting requirements.[402]
- One rule concerned the methods used for compilation and submission of data on state taxes that Class 1 railroads submitted annually to the STB for Revenue Shortfall Allocation Method (RSAM) computations.[403]

Analysis

Regulatory Flexibility Analysis

Waste Transfer Facilities Rule
The notice for the waste transfer facility rule included a certification that there would not be a significant impact on a substantial number of small entities. Although some of the formal elements of an initial regulatory flexibility analysis (particularly the number of small entities affected) were not included, there was a substantive discussion of the effects of the rule, and the discussion covered several key aspects of regulatory flexibility alternatives:

- Except for one provision,[404] a carrier is not required to obtain a land-use-exemption permit; it may operate under a state siting permit. In effect, the land-use-exemption permit provided a sort of regulatory alternative - an appeal to a state denial of a siting permit if the state requirements are "unduly burdensome to interstate commerce [or] discriminate against rail carriers."
- The regulation included a waiver provision to mitigate any significant negative impact on small entities.
- No alternative would adequately achieve the objectives of the Clean Railroads Act of 2008.

RSAM Rule
The RSAM notice contained neither any regulatory flexibility analysis nor a certification. The rule, however:

- Involved minor procedural changes that had minimal impacts; and
- Affected only Class 1 railroads – the seven largest U.S. rail carriers.[405]

Assessment
This very limited sample of rulemakings suggests that the STB understood and practiced the essence of regulatory flexibility, even if all the formalities were not observed.

End Notes

[1] 5 USC § 602.

[2] The Federal Election Commission (FEC), the Federal Housing Finance Agency (FHFA), the National Indian Gaming Commission (NIGC), the Postal Regulatory Commission (PRC), and the Recovery Accountability and Transparency Board (RATB).

[3] The Federal Mine Safety and Health Review Commission (FMSHRC) and the Occupational Safety and Health Review Commission (OSHRC).

[4] The National Labor Relations Board.

[5] The study was based on a review of final rules of independent federal agencies listed in the Unified Agenda for Spring 2010, Fall 2010, or Spring 2011.

[6] The Farm Credit Administration (FCA), the Federal Deposit Insurance Corporation (FDIC), the Federal Reserve System (FRS), the National Credit Union Administration (NCUA), the Commodity Futures Trading Commission (CFTC), and the Securities and Exchange Commission (SEC).

[7] The Consumer Product Safety Commission (CPSC) and the Nuclear Regulatory Commission (NRC).

[8] The Federal Communications Commission (FCC), the Federal Energy Regulatory Commission (FERC), the Federal Trade Commission (FTC), the Federal Maritime Commission (FMC), and the Surface Transportation Board (STB).

[9] The CFTC, FERC, and NRC.

[10] The FCA and FMC.

[11] The FCC, FCUA, STB, and SEC.

[12] Executive Order 12291, *Federal Regulation*, February 17, 1981.

[13] Executive Order 12866, *Regulatory Planning and Review*, September 30, 1993.

[14] Executive Order 13272, *Proper Consideration of Small Entities in Agency Rulemaking*, August 13, 2002.

[15] Executive Order 13563, *Improving Regulation and Regulatory Review*, January 18, 2011.

[16] 5 USC §§ 601-612. The Regulatory Flexibility Act was originally passed in 1980 (P.L. 96-354). The act was amended by the Small Business Regulatory Enforcement Fairness Act of 1996 (P.L. 104-121).

[17] The definition of "Agency" referenced in 5 USC § 601(1) excepts only Congress, courts, and governments of DC and territories.

[18] "The term 'rule' means any rule for which the agency publishes a general notice of proposed rulemaking pursuant to section 553(b) of this title, or any other law, including any rule of general applicability governing Federal grants to State and local governments for which the agency provides an opportunity for notice and public comment, except that the term "rule" does not include a rule of particular applicability relating to rates, wages, corporate or financial structures or reorganizations thereof, prices, facilities, appliances, services, or allowances therefore or to valuations, costs or accounting, or practices relating to such rates, wages, structures, prices, appliances, services, or allowances." (§ 601(2))

[19] 5 USC § 602.

[20] 5 USC § 603(b)

[21] 5 USC § 603(c).

[22] 5 USC § 604.

[23] 5 USC § 553. The APA provides some exemptions, including:

- Rules dealing with military or foreign affairs functions,

- Rules related solely to agency management or personnel, and
- Rules that are strictly interpretive or procedural.

[24] The key terms are defined in various ways:

- The SBA has published industry definitions of "small" (13 CFR 121 – also see www.sba.gov/size), and agencies may (after consulting the SBA) develop their own size standards.
- Rules of thumb have been developed for "significant." For depository institutions, for example, executive branch agencies have used a standard of 5 percent of labor costs or 2.5 percent of non-interest expenses.
- "Substantial" often is fairly obvious (e.g., 2,500 or 6) but gray areas should be considered substantial.

[25] Two other FCC rulemakings – the 2003 Triennial Review Order and the 2011 Open Internet ruler – were included to give a fuller picture.

[26] In some instances, the "completed action" was withdrawal of a rule or some other sort of notice. Most of the time "final action" meant that the final rule was not yet published, although some of these were included because they subsequently achieved "completed action" status

[27] 5 USC § 603 calls for:

- a succinct statement of the need for, and objectives of, the rule;
- a summary of the significant issues raised by the public comments in response to the initial regulatory flexibility analysis, a summary of the assessment of the agency of such issues, and a statement of any changes made in the proposed rule as a result of such comments;
- a description of and an estimate of the number of small entities to which the rule will apply or an explanation of why no such estimate is available;
- a description of the projected reporting, recordkeeping and other compliance requirements of the rule, including an estimate of the classes of small entities which will be subject to the requirement and the type of professional skills necessary for preparation of the report or record; and
- a description of the steps the agency has taken to minimize the significant economic impact on small entities consistent with the stated objectives of applicable statutes, including a statement of the factual, policy, and legal reasons for selecting the alternative adopted in the final rule and why each one of the other significant alternatives to the rule considered by the agency which affect the impact on small entities was rejected.

[28] The FERC could be included in this grouping, as it regulates forms of transportation, but its jurisdiction is broader.

[29] The STB is a successor to the Interstate Commerce Commission.

[30] These agencies are:

- The Federal Mine Safety and Health Review Commission (FMSHRC); see FMSHRC, p. 78; and
- The Occupational Safety and Health Review Commission (OSHRC); see OSHRC, p. 106.

[31] These agencies are:

- The Postal Regulatory Commission (PRC); see PRC, p. 107;
- The Federal Housing Finance Agency (FHFA); see FHFA, p. 74; and
- The Recovery Accountability and Transparency Board (RATB); see RATB, p. 108.

[32] These agencies are:
- The Federal Election Commission (FEC); see FEC, p. 66; and
- The National Indian Gaming Commission (NIGC); see NIGC, p. 100.

[33] These agencies are:
- The Farm Credit Administration (FCA),
- The Federal Deposit Insurance Corporation (FDIC),
- The Federal Reserve System (FRS), and
- The National Credit Union Administration (NCUA).

[34] These agencies are:
- The Commodity Futures Trading Commission (CFTC), and
- The Securities and Exchange Commission (SEC).

[35] These agencies are:
- The Federal Reserve System (FRS), and
- The Federal Trade Commission (FTC).

[36] These agencies are:
- The Federal Housing Finance Agency (FHFA), and
- The Recovery Accountability and Transparency Board (RATB).

[37] These agencies are:
- The Consumer Product Safety Commission (CPSC), and
- The Nuclear Regulatory Commission (NRC).

[38] These agencies are:
- The Federal Communications Commission (FCC),
- The Federal Energy Regulatory Commission (FERC),
- The Federal Trade Commission (FTC),
- The Federal Maritime Commission (FMC),
- The Surface Transportation Board (STB), and
- The National Labor Relations Board (NLRB). The NLRB had no final rules during the study period. See NLRB, p. 101.

[39] See FCA, p. 33.

[40] In CFTC parlance, they are "excluded from the definition of small." The CFTC does not have a size standard for entities in classes that have no asset registration, so that they could be both small and regulated. No regulations affecting such entities were found in this study. See CFTC, p. 20.

[41] The FERC regulates energy companies that operate intra-state only to the extent that the regulation is clearly necessary for a federal purpose or program. Only two FERC regulations in the study period affected intra-state entities, most of which are small. See FERC, pp. 71-72.

[42] These include:
- Self-regulating organizations (SROs) – i.e., stock exchanges, and non-SRO trading centers,
- Nationally Recognized Statistical Rating Organizations, and
- Recipients of TARP funds. See SEC, p. 113.

[43] For example:
- The SEC consistently provided relatively complete detail about compliance activities and was most likely to include some kind of regulatory flexibility measure.
- The Federal Reserve was relatively hesitant to commit to a certification and had relatively weak analyses.

- The NCUA was rather minimalist in its analysis, but most of its rules were minor.

[44] See FCC, pp. 39-44.

[45] The Federal Communications Commission, the Securities and Exchange Commission, and the Federal Reserve Board.

[46] The Federal Trade Commission and the National Credit Union Administration. The CPSC had four such regulations, but they were all mandated by the same statute and applied the same requirement to different products, so that the resulting analyses amounted to one analysis done four times with different names and numbers.

[47] This exemption was cited most often by the FERC (13 rules), NRC (5 rules), and CPSC, FDIC, and FMC (3 rules each). Various circumstances were described, the most common being:

- The rule applied only to internal agency procedures. See FERC, p. 70; FMC, p. 76; and SEC, p. 111.
- The rule made a correction ("ministerial" or otherwise). See FERC, p. 70 and NRC, p. 102.
- The rule was an interpretation of the statute. See CPSC, p. 26.
- The rule incorporated by reference regulations of another agency. See FDIC, p. 63.

[48] See FRS, p. 83.

[49] See FDIC, p. 63.

[50] See CPSC, p. 29.

[51] The most commonly cited reasons that impacts were not significant included:

- The rule made no changes, sometimes doing no more than extending existing rules.
- The rule simply provided clarification and/or definitions that were helpful.
- The rule gave regulated entities more operational flexibility, otherwise eased regulatory requirements, or withdrew another rule.
- The rule expanded the options available to the regulated entities.
- The rule was elective, not mandatory. This was true of most rules that created a form.
- The rule affected only internal regulatory procedures (so that an exemption might have been claimed).

[52] An NCUA rule that eliminated "RegFlex" exemptions was an apparent exception. It was not clear how many entities would be affected or what size they were. The NCUA devised a mechanism to cushion the impacts, however, and a NCUA representative opined that this rule would affect mostly large entities. See NCUA, p. 97.

The FCC, whose certification was meager and haphazard, is an exception. See FCC, p. 37.

[53] Two agencies, in particular, illustrate this tendency.

- The Federal Reserve sometimes expressed a belief (but did not certify) that impacts were not significant, reported a rather cursory and not very definitive FRFA, and then reached the (probably appropriate) conclusion of no significant impacts without really having provided much further basis. The FRS also illustrated inconsistency; it certified only one of two equally certifiable rules pertaining to the Community Reinvestment Act. See FRS, pp. 83-84.
- The FTC tended to make a certification and then include a brief FRFA as a check, "to explain the impacts of the amendments on small entities" (as one notice stated). See FTC, p. 92.

[54] The FCC's Triennial Review Order (2003) was an exception, in that the FCC was still grappling with implementation of Section 251 of the Telecommunications Act of 1996.

[55] The SEC lists eight statutes; the CPSC lists ten.

[56] The Dodd-Frank Act led to considerable reorganization of financial regulation, including creation of the Consumer Financial Protection Bureau (CFPB), but the CFPB is an executive agency and thus not part of this study.

[57] See, for example, CPSC, pp. 27-28; FRS, p. 84; and FTC, p. 92. The FCC, by contrast, often stated a policy goal. See FCC, pp. 37-38.

[58] The Consumer Product Safety Commission, for example, used industry data.

[59] Gift cards were a problem for the FRS (see FRS, p. 85). The FTC noted, "The [consumer finance] entities under the Commission's jurisdiction are so varied that there is no way to identify them in general and, therefore, no way to know how many of them qualify as small businesses." (see FTC, p. 93).

[60] Several agencies have adopted regulations that defined size standards of their own.
- The NCUA has a size standard for credit unions of $10 million in assets. (The corresponding SBA standard is $175 million.) See NCUA, p. 96.
- The CFTC has developed size standards for specific type of non-depository financial entity based on registration, the largest of which is $20 million. See CTFC, p. 20.
- The SEC has developed its own set of size standards for half a dozen types of entities, derived from various authorizing statutes. See SEC, p. 112.

[61] These included:
- Census data for six-digit NAICS industries,
- Data from auctions for FCC licenses (which were extremely fragmentary),
- Subscriber data for cable services, and
- Raw license counts.

[62] These included:
- SBA size standards,
- Size standards developed for FCC license auctions, and
- Statute-based size standards.

[63] See FCC, pp. 44-53.

[64] See FCC, pp. 51-53.

[65] FCC discussions were rarely more than a rather sparse, detached list of compliance activities; sometimes only a recap of provisions of the rule; and occasionally entirely generic. For example: "The rules adopted by this Report and Order impose reporting, recordkeeping and other compliance requirements on small entities." See FCC, pp. 53-55.

[66] Such estimates were made in Paperwork Reduction Act analysis, but these usually were averages across all sizes. A labeling rule by the FTC is one of the few instances of costs in a FRFA; see FTC, p. 93.

[67] For example: "The [Federal Reserve] Board notes that the precise costs to small entities to conform their open-end credit disclosures to the final rule and the costs of updating their systems to comply with the rule are difficult to predict. These costs depend on a number of factors that are unknown to the Board, including, among other things, the specifications of the current systems used by such entities to prepare and provide disclosures and administer credit card accounts, the complexity of the terms of the credit card products that they offer, and the range of such product offerings." See FRS, p. 86.

[68] See FRS, p. 86.

[69] A few Paperwork Reduction Act estimates were disaggregated by business size. See SEC, p. 114.

[70] The *Secure and Fair Enforcement for Mortgage Licensing (S.A.F.E.) Act* Rule was issued jointly by the FCA, FDIC, FRS, NCUA, Office of the Comptroller of the Currency, and Office of Thrift Supervision.

[71] The rule involved both initial costs and annual costs in subsequent years. Costs differed for institutions subject to the *de minimis* provisions and institutions subject to the full requirements of the rule.

- The FDIC estimated both types of costs for both classes of entities; computed the full-requirement costs as percentages of an average small institution's total non-interest costs; and concluded that impacts (0.7 percent initially and 0.3 percent thereafter) were not significant. See FDIC, p. 64.
- The Federal Reserve made a single cost estimate that covered all affected institutions and declared the impacts to be non-significant. See FRS, p. 88.
- The NCUA did not estimate compliance costs. See NCUA, pp. 98-99.
- The FCA did not do a regulatory flexibility analysis on the grounds that the cooperative system is one large entity. See FCA, p. 33.

[72] For example:

- The CPSC acknowledged that its safety standards could well have very serious impacts on some small entities that were too far out of compliance. Yet the standard essentially was statutory, and these were the cases where compliance was needed most. See CPSC, p. 27.
- The FERC was concerned that the full standards to safeguard critical cyber assets would impose heavy burdens of very small entities that had to comply with all the steps, but compliance in those cases was necessary for the objective of the regulation. The FERC was able to define a threshold, however, and it suggested some options to mitigate burdens. See FERC, p. 72.

[73] See FCC, pp. 43-44, 59.

[74] In several rules, the Federal Reserve used a cursory FRFA to confirm its belief that there were not significant impacts, and this lack of response seemed to be interpreted as confirmation. See FRS, p. 84.

[75] The explanation typically was that:

- The suggestion was contrary to statutory requirements,
- An exemption would compromise achievement of the rule's objective, or
- A provision in the regulation already addressed the issue adequately (or at least as well as the suggestion).

  The FCC, however, rarely discussed alternatives at all and rejected numerous suggestions with no real explanation.

[76] See, for example, CPSC, p. 30.

[77] See FTC, p. 92.

[78] See CPSC, p. 26.

[79] The *Privacy of Consumer Financial Information* Rule was issued jointly by the FDIC, FRS, FTC, NCUA, SEC, Office of the Comptroller of the Currency, and Office of Thrift Supervision.

[80] As the SEC put it in one rule, "the purpose of the rules is to facilitate the exercise of shareholders' traditional State law rights [and] we believe that shareholders of smaller reporting companies should be able to exercise these rights to the same extent as shareholders of larger reporting companies."

[81] See FTC, p. 93.

[82] See SEC, p. 115.

[83] See NCUA, p. 99.

[84] See FCC, p. 56.

[85] See FTC, p. 94.

[86] See SEC, pp. 115-116.

[87] See CPSC, p. 28.

[88] See SEC, p. 115.

[89] See FRS, p. 87 and FTC, p. 94.

[90] See NRC, p. 104.

[91] See FDIC, p. 65; FRS, p. 88; and FTC, p. 94.

[92] The joint model privacy notification, for example, underwent focus groups, field testing, and a variety of other developmental activities. The agencies developed Online Form Builder to minimize the burden on small businesses of developing, using, and customizing the model form for their individual needs.

[93] See FERC, p. 71.

[94] See SEC, p. 115.

[95] See FTC, p. 92.

[96] See FTC, p. 94.

[97] See SEC, p. 116.

[98] See CPSC, p. 27.

[99] See, for example, FRS, p. 88.

[100] See FERC, pp. 71-72.

[101] This overview is based primarily on information from the CTFC website.

[102] This includes one interim final rule that had no further action. Some rulemakings had more than one RIN.

[103] *Commodity Pool Operator Periodic Account Statements and Annual Financial Reports*, Final Action published November 9, 2009 (RIN: 3038-AC38).
Electronic Filing of Financial Reports and Notices, Final Action published December 30, 2009 (RIN: 3038-AB87).

[104] *Account Class*, Final Action published April 6, 2010 (RIN: 3038-AC94).
Operation in the Ordinary Course of a Commodity Broker in Bankruptcy, Final Action published July 30, 2010 (RIN: 3038-AC90).

[105] *Retail Off-Exchange Foreign Exchange Transaction Rules*, Final Action published September 10, 2010 (RIN: 3038-AC61).

[106] *Reporting and Recordkeeping for Post-Enactment Swaps*, Interim Final Rule published December 17, 2010 (RIN: 3038-AD29).

[107] *Privacy of Consumer Financial Information*, Final Action published December 1, 2009 (RIN: 3038-AC04).

[108] The other agencies participating in this rulemaking were the Office of the Comptroller of the Currency (OCC), the Federal Reserve System, the Federal Deposit Insurance Corporation (FDIC), the National Credit Union Administration (NCUA), the Office of Thrift Supervision (OTS), the Federal Trade Commission (FTC), and the Securities and Exchange Commission (SEC).

[109] 47 FR 18619.

[110] The minimum net capital standard is $1,000,000 for FCMs and $45,000 for IBs, but in practice the standard is often several times higher.

[111] As one notice states: "The Commission has previously determined that, based on the fiduciary nature of the FCM customer relationships, as well as the requirement that FCMs meet minimum financial requirements, FCMs should be excluded from the definition of small entity."

[112] IBs are less clear. Some notices refer to small IBs, while others treat them in the same manner as FCMs.

[113] *Account Class; Operation in the Ordinary Course of a Commodity Broker in Bankruptcy*, and *Electronic Filing of Financial Reports and Notices.*

[114] *Commodity Pool Operator Periodic Account Statements and Annual Financial Reports.*

[115] *Reporting and Recordkeeping for Post-Enactment Swaps.*

[116] *Retail Off-Exchange Foreign Exchange Transaction Rules.*

[117] FMCs could engage in retail forex transactions without registering as RFEDs, but they had to meet the $20 million standard.

[118] By definition, a small CPO has under $400,000 in assets, while the capital requirement for an RFED is $20 million.

[119] *Privacy of Consumer Financial Information.*

[120] The other agencies participating in this rulemaking were the Office of the Comptroller of the Currency (OCC), the Federal Reserve System, the Federal Deposit Insurance Corporation (FDIC), the National Credit Union Administration (NCUA), the Office of Thrift Supervision (OTS), the Federal Trade Commission (FTC), and the Securities and Exchange Commission (SEC).

[121] In the case of the retail off-exchange foreign exchange market, for example, a major concern was that the market had been largely unregulated.

[122] This overview is based primarily on information from the CPSC website.

[123] This count excluded four rules that did nothing but rescind the predecessor to a new regulation.

[124] *Safety Standard for Infant Bath Seats*, Final Rule published June 4, 2010 (RIN: 3041-AC60).
Safety Standard for Infant Walkers, Final Rule published June 21, 2010 (RIN: 3041-AC59).
Safety Standards for Full-Size Baby Cribs and Non-Full-Size Baby Cribs, Final Rule published December 28, 2010 (RIN: 3041-AC57).
Safety Standard for Toddler Beds, Final Rule published April 20, 2011 (RIN: 3041-AC82).

[125] *Third Party Accreditation for Testing of Infant Walkers Under 16 CFR part 1216, Safety Standard*, Notice of Requirements published June 21, 2010 (RIN: 3041-AC89).
Third Party Accreditation for Testing of Youth Carpets and Rugs Under 16 CFR part 1630, Standard for the Surface Flammability of Carpets and Rugs and part 1631, Standard for the Surface Flammability of Small Carpets and Rugs, Notice of Requirements published July 21, 2010 (RIN: 3041-AC99).
Third Party Accreditation for Testing of Vinyl Plastic Film Under 16 CFR part 1611, Standard for the Flammability of Vinyl Plastic Film, which sets a minimum standard for flammability of vinyl plastic film which are subject to the requirements of the Flammable Fabrics Act, Notice of Requirements published July 21, 2010 (RIN: 3041-AD02).
Third Party Accreditation for Testing of Youth Mattresses, Mattress Pads, and/or Mattress Sets Under 16 CFR parts 1632, Standard for the Flammability of Mattresses and Mattress Pads and/or 1633, Standard for the Flammability (Open Flame) of Mattress Sets, which set minimum standards for flammability under the Flammable Fabrics Act, Notice of Requirements published August 18, 2010 (RIN: 3041-AD00).
Third Party Accreditation for Testing of Children's Wearing Apparel Under 16 CFR part 1610, Standard for the Flammability of Clothing Textiles, which provides a test to determine whether such clothing and fabrics exhibit "rapid and intense burning" and therefore are highly flammable, Notice of Requirements published August 18, 2010 (RIN: 3041-AD03).
Third Party Accreditation for Testing of Youth All Terrain Vehicles Under 16 CFR part 1420, Requirements for All Terrain Vehicles, Notice of Requirements published August 27, 2010 (RIN: 3041-AD04).

Third Party Accreditation for Testing of Children's Sleepwear Under 16 CFR part 1615, Standard for the Flammability of Children's Sleepwear: Sizes 0 Through 6X and part 1616, Standard for the Flammability of Children's Sleepwear: Sizes 7 Through 14, which set minimum standards for flammability of children's sleepwear under the Flammable Fabrics Act, Notice of Requirements published November 19, 2010 (RIN: 3041-AD01).

[126] *Civil Penalty Factors,* Interim Final Rule September 1, 2009; Final Rule March 31, 2010 (RIN: 3041-AC52).

[127] *Interpretation of "Children's Product,"* Final Rule published October 14, 2010 (RIN: 3041-AC75).

Virginia Graeme Baker Pool and Spa Safety Act; Interpretation of Unblockable Drain, Final Interpretive Rule published April 27, 2010 RIN: 3041-AC96.

[128] *Children's Products Containing Lead; Exemptions for Certain Electronic Devices,* Final Rule published January 20, 2010 (RIN: 3041-AC70).

Bicycle Regulation Amendments, Final Rule published May 13, 2011 (RIN: 3041-AC95).

[129] *Product Registration for Durable Infant and Toddler Products,* Final Rule published December 29, 2009 (RIN: 3041-AC53).

Guidelines and Requirements for Mandatory Recall Notices, Final Rule published January 21, 2010 (RIN: 3041-AC54). *Publicly Available Consumer Product Safety Information Database,* Final Rule published December 9, 2010 (RIN: 3041-AC84).

[130] Possible modifications included increasing the rolling friction within the walker's wheels, reducing the walker weight, and refining the friction strip design, which the CPSC believed would change costs "only marginally."

[131] Most of industry claimed compliance, but the CPSC did not seem to want to rely on that.

[132] Third party conformity assessment bodies are not owned, managed, or controlled by a manufacturer or private labeler of a children's product to be tested by the third party conformity assessment body for certification purposes.

[133] A "firewalled" conformity assessment bodies is owned (at least a 10% share), managed, or controlled by a manufacturer or private labeler of a children's product to be tested by the third party conformity assessment body for certification purposes but which meets special statutory criteria.

[134] This provision appears to apply to foreign governments, but may also pertain to state governments.

[135] All firewalled conformity assessment bodies must submit to the CPSC copies of their training documents showing how employees are trained to notify the Commission immediately and confidentially of any attempt by the manufacturer, private labeler, or other interested party to hide or exert undue influence over the third party conformity assessment body's test results. The CPSC must formally accept the accreditation application of a third party firewalled conformity assessment body.

[136] The CPSIA permits accreditation of a third party conformity assessment body owned or controlled, in whole or in part, by a government if:

- To the extent practicable, manufacturers or private labelers located in any nation are permitted to choose conformity assessment bodies that are not owned or controlled by the government of that nation;
- The third party conformity assessment body's testing results are not subject to undue influence by any other person, including another governmental entity;
- The third party conformity assessment body is not accorded more favorable treatment than other third party conformity assessment bodies in the same nation who have been accredited;

- The third party conformity assessment body's testing results are accorded no greater weight by other governmental authorities than those of other accredited third party conformity assessment bodies; and
- The third party conformity assessment body does not exercise undue influence over other governmental authorities on matters affecting its operations or on decisions by other governmental authorities controlling distribution of products based on outcomes of the third party conformity assessment body's conformity assessments.

[137] Four are Farm Credit Banks; one is an Agricultural Credit Bank with slightly differing authority (including provision of international banking services).

[138] As of October 1, 2011, this included 81 Agricultural Credit Associations, 3 Federal Land Credit Associations, 1 Agricultural Credit Bank, and 4 Farm Credit Banks. Differences arise largely from the statute under which each type was organized.

[139] *The Secure and Fair Enforcement for Mortgage Licensing Act (2008)*. Final Rule published July 28, 2010 (RIN: 3052-AC52).

[140] *Organization; Funding and Fiscal Affairs, Loan Policies and Operations, and Funding Operations — Director Elections*, Final Action published December 10, 2009 (RIN: 3052-AC43).
Borrower Rights — Effective Interest Rates, Final Action published December 22, 2009; Notice of Effective Date published March 8, 2010 (RIN: 3052-AC45).
Technical Changes, Direct Final Rule published June 24, 2010, became effective September 27, 2010 (RIN: 3052-AC63).

[141] *Joint and Several Liability Reallocation*, Final Notice published October 20, 2010 (RIN: 3052-AC64).

[142] *Regulatory Burden*, Final Notice of Intent published October 26, 2009 (RIN: 3052-AC39).

[143] *Loan Policies and Operations — Loan Terms and Conditions*, Review completed December 30, 2009 (RIN: 3052- AC48).
Funding and Fiscal Affairs, Loan Policies and Operations, and Funding Operations — Cooperative Principles, Review completed January 31, 2010 (RIN: 3052-AC48).
Farmer Mac — Corporate Governance, Review completed April 4, 2010 (RIN: 3052-AC53).
Loan Policies and Operations — Shared Asset Risk Management, Review completed December 30, 2010 (RIN: 3052-AC59).

[144] As of December 2011, 15 reviews were under way and seven NPRMs were scheduled for 2012.

[145] The statement that "none of the FCA's existing regulations meet the definition of a 'significant regulatory action' under EO 12866" does require quantification, but that is not an estimate of any precision.

[146] This overview is based primarily on information from the FCC website.

[147] Federal Communications Commission, *Strategic Plan, 2009-2014*.

[148] Among the rulemakings reviewed, for example:
- The Triennial Review Order occurred in the seventh year of implementation of Section 251, and
- The order on Preserving the Open Internet repeatedly cited policy established six years earlier.

[149] One set of comments to the FCC raised issues with respect to six interrelated dockets pertaining to broadband access:
- CC Docket No. 01-337: Review of Regulatory Requirements for Incumbent LEC Broadband Telecommunications Services

- CC Docket No. 01-338: Review of the Section 251 Unbundling Obligations of Incumbent Local Exchange Carriers; Implementation of the Local Competition Provisions of the Telecommunications Act of 1996; Deployment of Wireline Services Offering Advanced Telecommunications Capability,
- CC Docket 02-33; Appropriate Framework for Access to the Internet Over Wireline Facilities,
- GN Docket No. 00-185: Inquiry Concerning High-Speed Access to the Internet Over Cable and Other Facilities,
- CS Docket No. 02-52: Appropriate Regulatory Treatment for Broadband Access to the Internet Over Cable Facilities, and
- CC Docket No. 02-39: Notice of Inquiry Concerning a Review of the Equal Access and Nondiscrimination Obligations Applicable to Local Exchange Carriers.

[150] Six other RINs were described as completed actions, but these were discarded because:

- Two referred only to orders that were covered in other rulemakings reviewed,
- Two were only rejections of petitions for reconsideration, and
- In two cases, the most recent order dated from 2002 or earlier.

[151] *Streamlining Earth Station Licensing Rules*, Final Rule published November 12, 2003 (RIN: 3060-AH60).

Significantly Viewed Out-of-Market Broadcast Stations, Final Rule published December 27, 2005 (RIN: 3060-AI56).

Wireless Operation of the 3650-3700 MHz Band, Final Rule published May 11, 2005; Memorandum Opinion & Order published July 25, 2007 (RIN: 3060-AI50).

Coordination Between the Non-Geostationary and Geostationary Satellite Orbit, Final Rule published April 5, 2010 (RIN: 3060-AI21).

Implementation of the Net 911 Improvement Act of 2008, Final Action published July 6, 2009 (RIN: 3060-AJ09).

[152] *Service Rules for the 698–806 MHz Band and Revision of the Commission's Rules Regarding Enhanced 911 Emergency Calling Systems, Hearing Aid-Compatible Telephones, and Public Safety Spectrum Requirements*, Final Rule published May 16, 2007; Final Rule published August 24, 2007; and Final Rule published May 2, 2008 (RIN: 3060-AI30).

[153] *Fixed Satellite Service and Terrestrial System in the Ku-Band*, Final Rule published February 16, 2001; Final Rule published June 26, 2002; Final Rule published May 18, 2004 (RIN: 3060-AH17).

Promotion of Spectrum Efficient Technologies on Certain Part 90 Frequencies[153] Final Rule published July 17, 2003; Final Rule published June 15, 2005; Final Rule published April 18, 2007 (RIN: 3060-AH33).

Spectrum Requirements for Advanced Medical Technologies, Final Rule published May 14, 2009; Final Rule published August 26, 2010 (RIN: 3060-AI76).

[154] *Air-Ground Telecommunications Services*, Final Rule published April 13, 2005 (RIN: 3060-AI27).

Promoting Efficient Use of Spectrum Through Elimination of Barriers to the Development of Secondary Markets, Final Rule published November 25, 2003; Final Rule published December 27, 2004; Final Rule published August 1, 2007 (RIN: 3060-AH82).

Rules Regarding Ultra-Wideband Transmission Systems, Final Rule (First Report & Order) published May 16, 2002; Memorandum Opinion and Order published April 22, 2003; Second Report & Order and Second Memorandum Opinion and Order published February 9, 2005; Third Report & Order and Third Memorandum Opinion and Order published October 12, 2010. (RIN: 3060-AH47).

[155] *Forbearance Procedures*, Final Action published August 6, 2009 (RIN: 3060-AJ31).
In the Matter of Procedural Amendments to Commission Part 1 Competitive Bidding Rules, Final Action published January 29, 2010 (RIN: 3060- AJ34).

[156] *DTV Consumer Education Initiative*, Order published March 24, 2008 (RIN: 3060-AI96).

[157] *Direct Broadcast Public Interest Obligations*, Final Rule published February 8, 1999; Order on Reconsideration published April 28, 2004 (RIN: 3060-AH59).

[158] *Preserving the Open Internet*, Final Rule published September 23, 2011 (RIN: 3060-AJ30).

[159] *Review of the Section 251 Unbundling Obligations of Incumbent Local Exchange Carriers, Implementation of the Local Competition Provisions of the Telecommunications Act of 1996, Deployment of Wireline Services Offering Advanced Telecommunications Capability*, CC Docket Nos. 01-338, 96-98, 98-147, Report and Order and Order on Remand and Further Notice of Proposed Rulemaking, 18 FCC Rcd 16978, 17145, para. 278 (2003) (Triennial Review Order)
Review of the Section 251 Unbundling Obligations of Incumbent Local Exchange Carriers, CC Docket No. 01- 338, Order on Remand.

[160] These included:

- More effectively accommodate the operation of implanted and body-worn medical transmitters,
- Facilitate the provision of service to consumers, especially those in rural areas, and encourage public safety services to use advanced wireless broadband communications capabilities,
- Increase competition and provided new high-speed data services to the public,
- "Promote and enhance public safety by facilitating the rapid deployment of IP-enabled 911 and E911 services, encourage the Nation's transition to a national IP-enabled emergency network, and improve 911 and enhanced 911 (E911) access to those with disabilities,"

[161] Of these rules:

- Three involved some aspect of reconfiguration of the spectrum,
- One sought to remove regulatory barriers and increase competition,
- One sought to increase efficiency of spectrum use through licensing changes, and
- One (that implemented deadline-mandated statutory requirements) enhanced satellite carriers' authority to offer signals.

[162] The goal of the controversial Open Internet rule was to "empower and protect consumers and innovators while helping ensure that the Internet continues to flourish, with robust private investment and rapid innovation at both the core and the edge of the network" by adopting "three basic rules that are grounded in broadly accepted Internet norms, as well as our own prior decisions:

i.   Transparency. Fixed and mobile broadband providers must disclose the network management practices, performance characteristics, and terms and conditions of their broadband services;

ii.   No blocking. Fixed broadband providers may not block lawful content, applications, devices, or non-harmful devices; mobile broadband providers may not block lawful Web sites, or block applications that compete with their voice or video telephony services; and

iii. No unreasonable discrimination. Fixed broadband providers may not unreasonably discriminate in transmitting lawful network traffic."

[163] These issues included the following:

- In a rule to develop secondary markets for spectrum use, the issue was whether eligibility rules applicable to a license should also be applied to secondary market lessees. The FCC responded that, although waiving these restrictions would open opportunities for small businesses, it would also invite circumvention of the underlying purposes of the rules, and that legal obligations and integrity of policies required the restrictions.
- In one rule, "the need to establish opportunities for smaller entities to have access to MVDDS spectrum was a sentiment expressed by commenters in the MVDDS rule making proceeding." Various smaller geographic and population areas were discussed and adopted in the rule.
- In one rule, comments generally noted costs and burdens of specific requirements.

[164] Specifically, the FCC stated that "it:

(1) has published a "notice of proposed rulemaking in publications likely to be obtained by small entities";

(2) has "included . . . a statement that the proposed rule may have a significant economic effect on a substantial number of small entities" in the Interim Order and NPRM;

(3) has solicited comments over its computer network; and

(4) has acted "to reduce the cost or complexity of participation in the rulemaking by small entities" by, among other things, facilitating electronic submission of comments."

[165] In part, this illustrates the problems inherent in providing illustrative examples of compliance activities. On the one hand, the examples may be interpreted as requirements. On the other hand (as here) they may be interpreted as a letter-of-the-law checklist of activities that satisfy all requirements, even if they are not adequate for the purpose of the requirement under various circumstances.

[166] The comments actually were phrased in terms of Executive Order 13272. As the FCC noted (without pressing the point), it is not subject to executive orders because it is an independent agency. Executive Order 13272, however, requires that agencies comply with the RFA – to which independent agencies are subject – both as a general statement and in a number of particulars.

[167] Thomas M. Sullivan, Eric E. Menge, and Radwan Saade, Ph. D. to Michael K. Powell, *RE: Ex Parte Presentation in a Non-Restricted Proceeding Initial Regulatory Flexibility Analysis for Triennial Review of Unbundled Network Elements (CC Dkt. No. 01-338; CC Dkt. No. 96-98; CC Dkt No. 98-147)*, February 5, 2003.

[168] In fact, every paragraph in the body of the NPRM (except the initial Background paragraph), as well as the paragraphs in the Description of Projected Requirements and Steps Taken to Minimize Impact sections of the IRFA, began with some variant of "the Commission seeks comment."

[169] U.S. Telecom Ass'n v. FCC, 290 F.3d 415 (D.C. Circuit, 2002).

[170] The FCC consistently showed a similar lack of initiative in not seeking Census data more disaggregated than the six-digit NAICS level or with more detailed size classes.

[171] *County Business Patterns* data are commonly used in regulatory flexibility analysis because they provide excellent detail on establishments by size class.

[172] A footnote added, "These include, for example, the essential facilities doctrine, an antitrust analysis, a market power analysis, and the approach to impairment the Commission took in the UNE Remand Order."

[173] Barriers to entry and issues related to small carriers' incentive and ability to invest in infrastructure - "Competitive LECs do not have the ability to recover sunk costs in self-

deploying DS1 loops" - were mentioned, almost in passing. Required notification by ILECs for planned retiring of copper loops was discussed at slightly greater length.

[174] "The agency shall prepare and make available for public comment an initial regulatory flexibility analysis. Such analysis shall describe the impact of the proposed rule on small entities." (§ 603(a))

[175] Michigan v. EPA, 213 F.3d 663, 689 (D.C. Cir. 2000) (internal quotation marks omitted);
Motor & Equip. Mfrs. Ass'n. v. Nichols, 142 F.3d 449, 467 (D.C. Cir. 1998);
United Distribution Cos. v. FERC, 88 F.3d 1105, 1170 (D.C. Cir. 1996);
American Trucking Assn's, Inc. v. EPA, 175 F.3d 1027, 1044, reh'g granted in part, denied in part 195 F.3d 4
(D.C. Cir. 1999), rev'd in part on other grounds, 531 U.S. 457 (2001).

[176] This interpretation appears only in Mid-Tex Electric Co-op Inc. v. F.E.R.C., 773 F.2d 327 (1985), which predates the other cases, but which the FCC did not cite.

[177] The version of this argument in the FRFA of the Triennial Review Order itself applied only to customers, clients, or end users. ISPs were added to the list when the argument was recycled in the Order on Remand FRFA.

[178] "In determining what network elements should be made available for purposes of subsection (c)(3), the Commission shall consider, at a minimum, whether... the failure to provide access to such network elements would impair the ability of the telecommunications carrier seeking access to provide the services that it seeks to offer."

[179] "Such analysis shall describe the impact of the proposed rule on small entities." (§ 603(a))
"Each initial regulatory flexibility analysis shall also contain a description of any significant alternatives to the proposed rule which accomplish the stated objectives of applicable statutes and which minimize any significant economic impact of the proposed rule on small entities." (§ 603(c))

[180] The FCC's industry groupings are identified in subsequent footnotes to the discussion of methodologies.

[181] This industry might be plausible if Broadband over power lines (BPL) were the basis for including it. This was hinted at, but not explained. Even so, the analysis should be limited Transmission and Distribution and not include Power Generation.

[182] For example: "We anticipate that some broadband service providers may not provide telephone service. Accordingly, we describe below other types of firms that may provide broadband services, including cable companies, MDS providers, and utilities, among others."

[183] For example:
- "While internet service providers (ISPs) are only indirectly affected by our present actions, and ISPs are therefore not formally included within this present FRFA, we have addressed them informally to create a fuller record and to recognize their participation in this proceeding."
- "While these [software publishing] entities are merely indirectly affected by our action, we are describing them to achieve a fuller record."
- "The SBA's Office of Advocacy contends that, for RFA purposes, small incumbent LECs are not dominant in their field of operation because any such dominance is not 'national' in scope. We have therefore included small incumbent LECs in this RFA analysis, although we emphasize that this RFA action has no effect on Commission analyses and determinations in other, non-RFA contexts."

[184] This was generally the latest Economic Census for which data were available, but in a number of instances data were not updated from an earlier Economic Census.

[185] Industries appearing in at least on rulemaking and their NAICS codes (2007, except where noted) were:
- Software Publishers (NAICS 511210),
- Radio Networks (NAICS 515111),
- Radio Stations (NAICS 515112),
- Television Broadcasting (NAICS 515120),
- Cable and Other Subscription Programming (NAICS 515210),
- Wired Telecommunications Carriers (NAICS 517110),
- Wireless Telecommunications Carriers (except Satellite) (NAICS 517210),
- Paging (2002 NAICS 517211),
- Cellular and Other Wireless Telecommunications (2002 NAICS 517212),
- Satellite Telecommunications (NAICS 517410),
- Telecommunications Resellers (NAICS 517911),
- All Other Telecommunications (NAICS 517919),
- Internet Service Providers (2002 NAICS 518111),
- Web Search Portals (2002 NAICS 518112),
- Data Processing, Hosting, and Related Services (NAICS 518210),
- Internet Publishing and Broadcasting (2002 NAICS 516110), and
- All Other Information Service (NAICS 519190).

[186] Industries appearing in at least on rulemaking and their NAICS codes (2007, except where noted) were:
- Electric Power Generation, Transmission and Distribution (2002 NAICS 2211),
- Radio and Television Broadcasting and Wireless Communications Equipment Manufacturing (NAICS 334220),
- Electronic Computer Manufacturing (NAICS 334111),
- Computer Storage Device Manufacturing (NAICS 334112),
- Computer Terminal Manufacturing (NAICS 334113),
- Other Computer Peripheral Equipment Manufacturing (NAICS 334119),
- Audio and Video Equipment Manufacturing (NAICS 334310),
- Electron Tube Manufacturing (NAICS 334411),
- Bare Printed Circuit Board Manufacturing (NAICS 334412),
- Semiconductor and Related Device Manufacturing (NAICS 334413),
- Electronic Capacitor Manufacturing (NAICS 334414),
- Electronic Resistor Manufacturing (NAICS 334415),
- Electronic Coil, Transformer, and Other Inductor Manufacturing (NAICS 334416)
- Electronic Connector Manufacturing (NAICS 334417),
- Printed Circuit Assembly (Electronic Assembly) Manufacturing (NAICS 334418)
- Other Electronic Component Manufacturing (NAICS 334419),
- Radio, Television and Other Electronics Stores (NAICS 443112),
- Electronic Shopping (NAICS 454111), and
- Custom Computer Programming Services (NAICS 541511).

[187] Just before making the estimate, the FCC stated that (because of stringent FDA approval requirements) this is a "highly specialized market niche" and estimated that five to ten manufacturers produce the devices in question. The FCC then went on to estimate the number of small entities on the basis of six-digit NAICS data.

[188] Except for All Other Telecommunications ($25 million), current SBA revenue size standards in these subsectors are $7 million, $14 million, or $15 million. Census data size classes break at $5 million, $10 million, and $25 million. Thus the FCC generally provided either:

- The numbers of entities with less than $5 million in revenues and with $5 million but less than $10 million, or
- The numbers of entities with less than $10 million in revenues and with $10 million but less than $25 million. Similarly the SBA employment size standard is 1,500, and the nearest break in Census data is 1,000 employees. Here the FCC provided the numbers of entities with less than 1,000 employees and with 1,000 or more employees.

[189] Recent County Business Pattern data indicate that 61 percent of all establishments with employees have fewer than five employees; 89 percent have fewer than 20 employees; and 99.7 percent have fewer than 500 employees.

[190] Data for industry groups in NAICS 517110 were cited in one of the earliest rules as being from *Trends in Telephone Service* (a compilation of FCC data). BIA Publications, *Master Access Television Analyzer Database* was cited as the source of data for Television Broadcasting in one rule. Other sources were not identified.

[191] The industry groupings (as most often named in the analyses) and the NAICS industry from which each SBA size standard was taken were:

- Wireless Cable Systems – BRS/MDS (NAICS 515120),
- Television Broadcasting (NAICS 515120),
- Incumbent Local Exchange Carriers (ILECs) (NAICS 517110),
- Competitive Local Exchange Carriers (CLECs) (NAICS 517110),
- Prepaid Calling Card Providers (NAICS 517110),
- Other Toll Carriers (NAICS 517110),
- Interexchange Carriers (IXCs) (NAICS 517110),
- Operator Service Providers (OSPs) (NAICS 517110),
- Internet Service Providers (NAICS 517110 and 517919),
- Wireless Telephony (NAICS 517212),
- Local Resellers (NAICS 517911),
- Toll Resellers (NAICS 517911),
- Prepaid Calling Card Providers (NAICS 517911),
- 800 and 800-Like Service Subscribers (NAICS 517911),
- International Service Providers – Satellite Telecommunications (NAICS 517410),
- International Service Providers - All Other Telecommunications (NAICS 517919), and
- Public Safety (small municipal governments).

[192] The FCC computed this number from the actual standard of 1 percent of subscribers, nationwide.

[193] This approach was used for:

- Direct Broadcast Satellite (DBS) Service (NAICS 515210), and
- 24 GHz—Incumbent Licensees (NAICS 517212).

[194] Educational Broadband Service (EBS).

[195] Such an estimate was made in at least one rulemaking for:

- Class A TV, LPTV, and TV translator stations (NAICS 515120),
- Rural Radiotelephone Service (NAICS 517212),
- Air-Ground Radiotelephone Service (NAICS 517212),
- Aviation and Marine Radio Services (NAICS 517212),
- Offshore Radiotelephone Service (NAICS 517212), and

- Fixed Microwave Services (NAICS 517212).

196 These auctions included licenses for:

- Broadband Personal Communications Services,
- Narrowband Personal Communications Services,
- 39 GHz Service,
- Wireless Cable Systems – BRS/MDS,
- Wireless Cable Systems – LMDS,
- Local Multipoint Distribution Service,
- Wireless Communications Services (2305-2320 MHz and 2345-2360 MHz Bands),
- Lower 700 MHz Band, and
- Government Transfer Bands.

197 These auctions included licenses for:

- Paging,
- 220 MHz Radio Service—Phase II Licensees,
- Specialized Mobile Radio Licenses (800 MHz and 900 MHz),
- 700 MHz Guard Band Licenses,
- 218–219 MHz Service,
- Multiple Address Systems,
- Location and Monitoring Services,
- Aviation and Marine Radio Services, and
- AWS Services.

198 These auctions included licenses for:

- 1670-1675 MHz Band,
- Multichannel Video Distribution and Data Services,
- Upper 700 MHz Band, and
- Air-Ground Radiotelephone Service.

199 In one of the few instances where the FCC independently estimated the number of current licensees, the FCC reported that 61 small businesses had won licenses in the auction, while estimating that there were 440 small licensees.

200 For Broadband Personal Communications Service in the Preserving the Open Internet analysis, the FCC reported:

- Two auctions of C-Block licenses, where 90 small businesses won licenses,
- An auction of C-, D-, and F-Block licenses, where 93 small businesses won 40% of 1,479 licenses,
- An auction for C-, D-, E-, and F-Block licenses, where 48 of 57 winners were small businesses who won 277 of 347 licenses awarded,
- An auction of C-, D-, E-, and F-Block licenses, where 48 of 57 winners were small businesses who won 277 of 347 licenses awarded,
- An auction of 422 C- and F-Block licenses, where 29 of 35 winners were small businesses,
- An auction of C-, D-, E-, and F-Block licenses, where 16 of 24 winners were small businesses who won 156 licenses,
- An auction of A-, C-, F-Block licenses, where 5 of 12 winners were small businesses who won 18 licenses (although the FCC noted that "no small business within the SBA approved small business standards bid successfully for licenses in Blocks A and B"), and

- An auction of C-, D-, E-, and F-Block licenses, where 6 of 8 winners were small businesses who won 14 licenses.

[201] This occurred for:

- Open Video Systems (OVS) (NAICS 515210),
- Fixed-Satellite Service ("FSS") (515210),
- Private Cable Operators (PCOs) (515210),
- Home Satellite Dish (HSD) Service (NAICS 515210),
- Personal Radio Services (NAICS 515210),
- Private Land Mobile Radio (NAICS 517212).

[202] This occurred for:

- Upper 700 MHz Band,
- Advanced Wireless Transfer Bands, and
- 24 GHz—Future Licensees.

[203] 3650-3700 MHz Band.

[204] Electric Power Generation, Transmission and Distribution (2002 NAICS 2211).

[205] For 220 MHz Radio Service, for example, the FCC used standards of:

- 1,500 employees for Phase I licensees, and
- $15 million in revenues for Phase II licensees.

[206] "We do not know how many firms [that] provide 800 MHz or 900 MHz geographic area SMR service... have annual revenues of no more than $15 million [the FCC auction-based standard]. In addition, we do not know how many of these firms have 1,500 or fewer employees, which is the SBA-determined size standard."

[207] This did not always occur, because sometimes the NAICS industry was merely introduced as a sort of heading.

[208] Instances of this sort of double-counting included:

- Counting 2002 NAICS 517211 data as both Wireless Service Providers and Common Carrier Paging,
- Counting 2002 NAICS 517212 data as both Wireless Service Providers and 220 MHz Radio Service Phase I licensees, and
- Counting 1997 NAICS 517212 data as both 220 MHz Radio Service Phase I licensees and 24 GHz licensees.

[209] Under 2007 NAICS definitions, Wireless Communications Services (except Satellite) is NAICS 517210; Paging is NAICS 5172101; and Cellular and Other Wireless Communications is NAICS 5172102.

[210] The Open Internet analysis appeared to use seven-digit 2007 data for ISPs, although the FCC did not document this and the numbers cited did not match the published Census totals.

[211] Examples of such data include the Census Bureau's County Business Patterns and special tabulations prepared by the Census Bureau for SBA.

[212] One source was documented in one analysis.

[213] Examples of this sort of "Groundhog Day" effect include:

- There were always "presently approximately 55 licensees in [the offshore radiotelephone] service," and the FCC was always "unable at this time to estimate the number of licensees that would qualify as small entities."
- After repeatedly identifying Competitive Access Providers (CAPs), Shared-Tenant Service Providers, and Other Local Service Providers as specific types of Competitive LECs, the FCC never did anything with this information.

[214] For example:

- Upon request from a public safety entity, commercial licensees must provide the location and parameters of any station in the entity's area of operation.
- Applicants for MVDDS licenses were required to submit an FCC Form 175.

[215] For example:

- The immediate processing and immediate approval processes require "certain additional certifications."
- The relocation of public safety narrowband operations in the consolidated channels will entail some additional reporting, recordkeeping and compliance efforts by existing public safety entities.
- "While this Order imposes no general obligations on competitive LECs, the Order does require competitive LECs to satisfy certain reporting requirements in order to obtain as UNEs certain high-capacity network elements from incumbent LECs."

[216] For example: "The rules adopted by this Report and Order impose reporting, recordkeeping and other compliance requirements on small entities. The Report and Order establishes rules requiring industry to participate in a coordinated, nationwide, consumer outreach campaign."

[217] For example: "CMRS providers (except MSS) must comply with the 911/E911 requirements to the extent that they offer real-time, two way switched voice service that is interconnected with the public switched network and utilize an in-network-switching facility that enables the provider to reuse frequencies and accomplish seamless hand-offs of subscriber calls."

[218] In one rule involving a band that had only one large licensee, however, this appeared to be pure boilerplate: We do not anticipate any adverse impact on small entities resulting from either reconfiguration of the 800 MHz Air-Ground Radiotelephone Service band plan or revision of the related service rules.

[219] "In this Order, we determine that requesting carriers are impaired without

- access to local circuit switching in providing service to mass market customers using DS0 capacity loops...
- unbundled access to the incumbent LEC's 911 and e911 databases...
- access to incumbent LECs' OSS...
- access to copper loop or subloop facilities (and must condition copper loops for provision of advanced services)...
- access to unbundled subloops associated with accessing customer premises wiring at multiunit premises and are also impaired without unbundled access to the incumbent LEC Inside Wire Subloops and NIDs, regardless of loop type [and]
- access to unbundled shared transport only to the extent they are impaired without access to local circuit switching."

"In this Order, we determine that requesting carriers... are presumed not impaired without access to unbundled local circuit switching for the enterprise market [and] are not impaired without

- access to packet switching, including routers and DSLAMs...
- access to incumbent LECs' signaling systems except where they are also impaired without access to the incumbent LEC's unbundled circuit switching...
- access to the incumbent LEC's other call-related databases if they deploy their own switches, but otherwise are impaired...
- access to line-sharing (subject to a three-year transition) or hybrid loops...
- access to new build/greenfield fiber-to-the-home (FTTH) loops for broadband or narrowband services or overbuild/brownfield FTTH loops for broadband services...

- unbundled access to OCn capacity loop facilities, but are impaired, subject to certain triggers, without access to dark fiber loops, DS1 loops, and DS3 loops...
- unbundled access to OCn transport facilities, but are impaired, subject to certain triggers, without access to dark fiber transport facilities, DS1 transport facilities, and DS3 transport facilities."

[220] "Broadband providers must, at a minimum, prominently display or provide links to disclosures on a publicly available, easily accessible Web site that is available to current and prospective end users and edge providers as well as to the Commission, and at the point of sale. Providers should ensure that all Web site disclosures are accessible by persons with disabilities."

[221] The rule would require "professional skills of entering information onto a Web page and an understanding of the entities' network practices, both of which are easily managed by staff of these types of small entities."

[222] Three rules had no regulatory flexibility analysis; two stated that there were no costs for small entities; and one stated "the SHVERA [Satellite Home Viewer Extension and Reauthorization Act of 2004] did not offer much flexibility with respect to minimizing its impact on small entities... Therefore, the Commission does not have discretion to choose an alternate means of implementing the SHVERA."

[223] Elements of flexibility cited in this manner included:

- The FCC, noting that it had streamlined license requirements to reduce costs, stated: "The costs involved in the selection and use of frequencies by affected entities, including small entities, should be minimal because of the available on-line database to assist with these efforts."
- "We believe that the rules and policies we adopt will benefit all parties, including small entities, that would like to lease their spectrum to others or obtain additional spectrum for their own use. Small entities, like all covered entities, will be governed by reduced filing requirements and reduced regulatory uncertainty."
- The basic objective for the rule was "to provide adequate spectrum sharing criteria to minimize the potential for interference of these new NGSO FSS operations on incumbent operations, many of which qualify as small entities."
- "The Commission considered but declined to issue highly detailed rules [because] overly specific rules would fail to reflect these local variations, thereby placing undue burdens on all entities, including any small entities, involved in providing E911 service."
- "In this Order, we adopt a streamlined earth station application form designed to reduce the economic impact on all earth station applicants, including small entities."
- The FCC extended deadlines for all regulated entities, and in this case one of several considerations was "resources available to small entities."
- In the Open Internet rule, several aspects of the rule that would mitigate costs were cited:
  - The rule required only posting requirements on a Web site and at the point of sale,
  - There was flexibility about what information to disclose,
  - Setting a future effective date "gives broadband providers - including small entities - sufficient time and flexibility to implement the rules in a cost-effective manner."

- "These rules provide certainty and clarity that are beneficial... to broadband providers."
[224] Benefits of this sort included:
- Simply establishing procedures generally benefitted small entities by establishing the playing field and protecting them against "scattershot arguments that have been made by much larger entities."
- In the Consumer Education Initiative rule, in addition to several features of general benefit:
    - Small MVPDs could use electronic and automatic billing instead of printing "bill stuffer" transition notices.
    - "Most importantly, although these requirements will impose some costs on small broadcasters, they will also ensure that small broadcasters continue to retain their audiences after the transition by fully informing viewers of the steps necessary to keep watching. Small broadcasters rely completely on their viewing audience for their revenue stream, so this benefit should far outweigh any costs for this temporary requirement."
- In another rule:
    - The band plan will generally increase the opportunity of small businesses to gain licenses.
    - Small businesses will benefit from the mix of service areas (to be auctioned) that includes small geographic license areas.
    - "Partitioning and disaggregation allow smaller or newly-formed entities to enter the market for the first time, because they will be able to negotiate for portions of original licenses at costs that are proportionately less than the entire license."
    - "We believe that the open platform requirement for devices and applications will provide additional opportunities for small entities to participate in the device and application market"
    - Anonymous bidding will prevent retaliatory bidding and other practices that deter new entrants.
    - "The Commission believes that the interoperable broadband network will be of benefit to smaller governmental entities that would otherwise be unlikely to have the resources to construct such a network."
[225] These measures were:
- Auction bidding credits were adopted for entrepreneurs (15 percent), small businesses (25 percent), and very small businesses (35 percent). This was a standard FCC auction procedure, not specific to this rule.
- Small service areas (Component Economic Areas) were adopted for MVDDS, and partitioning of these service areas was permitted, so as to encourage smaller entities to participate in MVDDS auctions.
[226] "While we recognize that regulatory requirements may disproportionately impact smaller entities, we have adopted the least burdensome of several available alternatives in requiring competitors to satisfy certain service eligibility criteria. For example, rather than requiring carriers to certify to be the sole provider of local service in order to access certain elements (e.g., high-capacity loops and transport) – an approach that might require frequent and costly assurance from a carrier's customers – we permit carriers to certify that they are the primary providers of local service... We also adopt collocation and local interconnection requirements as less burdensome ways of assuring service eligibility. By contrast, we have

rejected a number of suggested approaches as unnecessarily burdensome, such as measuring minutes or traffic percentages, separately measuring voice and data use, or permitting UNEs only where a competitive carrier uses certain types of switches."

[227] "In determining what network elements should be made available for purposes of subsection (c)(3), the Commission shall consider, at a minimum, whether... the failure to provide access to such network elements would impair the ability of the telecommunications carrier seeking access to provide the services that it seeks to offer."

[228] For example: "We considered and rejected arguments that small competitive LECs are impaired in specific circumstances due to unique characteristics of the particular customer markets or geographic markets they seek to serve or because of the competitive carrier's size. For instance, some commenters argued that competitive LECs are uniquely impaired when seeking to serve rural areas. We concluded that these commenters' claims were at odds with our impairment standard, which evaluates impairment based on a 'reasonably efficient competitor,' not based on the individualized circumstances of a particular requesting carrier, and 'consider[s] all the revenue opportunities that such a competitor can reasonably expect to gain over the facilities, from providing all possible services that an entrant could reasonably expect to sell.'

[229] For example: "We recognize that the use restrictions adopted in this Order may prevent small providers of mobile wireless and long distance service from using UNEs to compete."

[230] SBA Office of Advocacy, *A Guide for Government Agencies: How to Comply with the Regulatory Flexibility Act*, June 2010.

[231] *United States Telecom Ass'n v. FCC*, 290 F.3d 415 (D.C. Cir. 2002) (USTA I).

[232] This overview is based primarily on information from the FDIC website.

[233] Some rulemakings had more than one RIN for the final rule or a separate RIN for an interim final rule.

[234] *Designated Reserve Ratio*, Final Rule published December 20, 2010 (RIN: 3064-AD69).

[235] *Prepaid Assessments*, Final Rule published November 17, 2009 (RIN: 3064-AD51).

[236] *Assessments, Assessment Base and Rates, and Large Bank Pricing*, Final Action published February 25, 2011 (RIN: 3064-AD66).

[237] *Temporary Increase in Standard Coverage Amount; Revocable Trust Accounts; Mortgage Servicing Accounts; Deposit Insurance Regulations; International Banking; Foreign Banks*, Final Action published September 17, 2009 (RIN: 3064-AD36).
Deposit Insurance Regulations; Permanent Increase in Standard Coverage Amount; Advertisement of Membership; International Banking; Foreign Banks, Final Rule published September 13, 2010 (RIN: 3064-AD61).

[238] In addition to the FDIC, the agencies included the Federal Reserve System, the Office of the Comptroller of the Currency (Treasury), and the Office of Thrift Supervision (Treasury).

[239] *Community Reinvestment Act Regulations*, Final Action published October 4, 2010 (RIN: 3064-AD45). *Community Reinvestment Act Regulations*, Final Rule published December 20, 2010 (RIN: 3064-AD60).

[240] *Community Reinvestment Act Regulations* Final Rule published December 14, 2009 (RIN: 3064-AD54). Final Rule published December 14, 2010 (RIN: 3064-AD68).

[241] *Impact of Modifications to Generally Accepted Accounting Principles; Risk-Based Capital Guidelines; Capital Adequacy Guidelines; Capital Maintenance: Regulatory Capital; Consolidation of Asset-Backed Commercial Paper Programs*, Final Rule published January 28, 2010 (RIN: 3064-AD48). Other agencies participating in this rulemaking included the Federal Reserve System, the Office of the Comptroller of the Currency (Treasury), and the Office of Thrift Supervision (Treasury).

[242] *Transitional Safe Harbor Protection for Treatment by the Federal Deposit Insurance Corporation as Conservator or Receiver of Financial Assets Transferred by an Insured Depository Institution in Connection With a Securitization or Participation*, Final Action published March 18, 2010 (RIN: 3064-AD55).

[243] *Deposit Insurance Regulations; Unlimited Coverage for Noninterest-bearing Transaction Accounts; Inclusion of Interest on Lawyers Trust Accounts*, Final Rule published November 15, 2010 (RIN: 3064-AD65); Final Rule published January 27, 2011 (RIN: 3064-AD72).

[244] *Privacy of Consumer Financial Information*, Final Action published December 1, 2009 (RIN: 3064-AD16). Other agencies participating in this rulemaking included the Federal Reserve System, the National Credit Union Administration (NCUA), the Securities and Exchange Commission (SEC), the Commodity Futures Trading Commission (CFTC), the Federal Trade Commission (FTC), and the Office of Thrift Supervision (Treasury).

[245] *S.A.F.E. Mortgage Licensing Act*, Final Rule published July 28, 2010 (RIN: 3064-AD43). Other agencies participating in this rulemaking included the Federal Reserve System, the National Credit Union Administration (NCUA), the Farm Credit Administration (FCA), the Office of the Comptroller of the Currency (Treasury), and the Office of Thrift Supervision (Treasury).

[246] *Minimum Capital Ratios; Capital Adequacy Guidelines; Capital Maintenance; Capital: Deduction of Goodwill Net of Associated Deferred Tax Liability*, Final Rule published December 30, 2008 (RIN: 3064-AD32). Other agencies participating in this rulemaking included the Federal Reserve System, the Office of the Comptroller of the Currency (Treasury), and the Office of Thrift Supervision (Treasury).

[247] *Interest Rate Restrictions on Institutions That Are Less Than Well Capitalized*, Final Action published December 3, 2009 (RIN: 3064-AD41).

[248] *Securities of Nonmember Insured Banks* Interim Final Rule published November 30, 2010 (RIN: 3064-AD67).

[249] *Risk-Based Capital Guidelines; Capital Adequacy Guidelines; Capital Maintenance; Capital—Residential Mortgage Loans Modified Pursuant to the Making Home Affordable Program*, Final Rule published December 21, 2009 (RIN: 3064-AD42).

[250] *Orderly Liquidation Authority Provisions of the Dodd-Frank Wall Street Reform and Consumer Protection Act*, Interim Final Rule published January 5, 2011 (RIN: 3064-AD73).

[251] "Certain types of rules, such as rules of particular applicability relating to rates or corporate or financial structures, or practices relating to such rates or structures, are expressly excluded from the definition of 'rule' for purposes of the RFA."

[252] For assessing impacts on liquidity, assessments were compared to current cash and cash equivalent reserves. Interest foregone was compared to projected interest earnings over the period (less than 0.05 percent).

[253] The FDIC's concise style is illustrated by the rule requiring revised official signs for an increase in the standard maximum insurance amount: "There would not be any compliance costs with displaying the [new] official sign, because it would be provided by the FDIC free of charge."

[254] The exception applied to any employee "who has never been registered or licensed through the Registry as a mortgage loan originator if during the past 12 months the employee acted as a mortgage loan originator for 5 or fewer residential mortgage loans."

[255] FDIC estimates were as follows:
- Banks subject only to *de minimis* requirements would incur cost of:
  - $12,922 for set-up and
  - $4,473 annually.

- Banks subject to full requirements would incur cost of:
  - $17,379 (0.7% of total non-interest costs) for set-up and
  - $7,436 (0.3% of total non-interest costs) annually.

[256] Examples include rules that:
- Made an increase in the standard minimum deposit insurance amount permanent and mandated new signage,
- Revised CRA size definitions, based on the CPI,
- Made assessment changes within a pre-existing risk-based assessment system,
- Temporarily extended existing regulations,
- Incorporated regulations of another agency by cross-referencing.

[257] The best example was the rule on a privacy notice model form, where the statute's mandate for a single standardized form precluded different treatment for small businesses. This form, however, was not mandatory.

[258] These included rules that:
- Provided new options for CRA assessment consideration,
- Facilitated participation in a HUD program, and
- The privacy notice model form.

[259] This overview is based primarily on information from the FEC website.

[260] This overview is based primarily on information from the FERC website.

[261] Specific responsibilities include:
- Approval of rates for wholesale sales of electricity and transmission in interstate commerce for jurisdictional utilities, power marketers, power pools, power exchanges and independent system operators,
- Review of rates set by the federal power marketing administrations,
- Review of exempt wholesale generator status, and
- Certification of qualifying small power production and cogeneration facilities.

[262] Specific responsibilities include:
- Regulation of rates and practices of oil pipeline companies engaged in interstate transportation;
- Establishment of equal service conditions to provide shippers with equal access to pipeline transportation; and
- Establishment of reasonable rates for transporting petroleum and petroleum products by pipeline.

[263] *Delegation for Notices of Penalty*, Final Rule published November 5, 2009 (RIN: 1902-AD91).
Instant Final Rule Transferring Certain Enforcement Hotline Matters to the Dispute Resolution Service, Final Rule published April 26, 2010 (RIN: 1902-AE08).
Delegations to Office of Energy Policy and Innovation, Final Rule published June 9, 2010 (RIN: 1902-AE09). *Delegations to Office of Energy Policy and Innovation*, Final Rule published July 26, 2010 (RIN: 1902-AE10). *Submissions to the Commission Upon Staff Intention to Seek an Order To Show Cause*, Final Rule published May 21, 2008 (RIN: 1902-AD65).
Service of Interlocutory Appeals, Final Rule published August 14, 2009 (RIN: 1902-AD93).
Supplemental Standards of Ethical Conduct for Employees of the Federal Energy Regulatory Commission, Final Rule published January 10, 2011 (RIN: 1902-AE29).

[264] *Modification of Interchange and Transmission Loading Relief Reliability Standards and Electric Reliability Organization Interpretation of Specific Requirements of Four Reliability*

Standards, Final Rule published July 28, 2008; Final Rule published March 24, 2009 (RIN: 1902-AD58).

Western Electricity Coordinating Council Regional Reliability Standard Regarding Automatic Time Error Correction, Final Rule published May 28, 2009 (RIN: 1902-AD67).

Electric Reliability Organization Interpretations of Specific Requirements of Frequency Response and Bias and Voltage and Reactive Control Reliability Standards, Final Rule published May 28, 2009 (RIN: 1902-AD69).

Mandatory Reliability Standards for the Calculation of Available Transfer Capability, Capacity Benefit Margins, Transmission Reliability Margins, Total Transfer Capability, and Existing Transmission Commitments and Mandatory Reliability Standards for the Bulk-Power System, Final Rule published December 8, 2009 (RIN: 1902- AD76).

Revised Mandatory Reliability Standards for Interchange Scheduling and Coordination, Final Rule published December 24, 2009 (RIN: 1902-AD80).

Version One Regional Reliability Standard for Resource and Demand Balancing, Final Rule published October 20, 2010 (RIN: 1902-AE05).

NERC is the Commission-certified electric reliability organization (ERO).

[265] *Annual Update of Filing Fees*, Final Rule published July 30, 2009 (RIN: 1902-AD85). *Annual Update of Filing Fees*, Final Rule published February 25, 2010 (RIN: 1902-AD90). *Annual Update of Filing Fees*, Final Rule published February 22, 2011 (RIN: 1902-AE27). *Natural Gas Pipelines; Project Cost and Annual Limits*, Final Rule published February 24, 2010 (RIN: 1902-AD99). *Natural Gas Pipelines; Project Cost and Annual Limits*, Final Rule published February 14, 2011 (RIN: 1902-AE28). *Interest Rates for Refunds*, Final Rule published October 22, 2009 (RIN: 1902-AD98).

[266] *Sales of Electric Power to the Bonneville Power Administration; Revisions to Average System Cost*, Final Rule published September 15, 2009 (RIN: 1902-AD72).

[267] *Standards for Business Practices of Interstate Natural Gas Companies*, Final Rule published March 3, 2009 (RIN: 1902-AD68).

Standards for Business Practices for Interstate Natural Gas Pipelines, Final Rule published April 9, 2010 (RIN: 1902-AD87).

Standards for Business Practices and Communication Protocols for Public Utilities, Final Rule published December 3, 2009 (RIN: 1902-AD79).

Standards for Business Practices and Communication Protocols for Public Utilities, Final Rule published April 22, 2010 (RIN: 1902-AD94).

[268] *Pipeline Posting Requirements Under Section 23 of the Natural Gas Act*, Final Rule published December 2, 2008 (RIN: 1902-AD49).

Revised Filing Requirements for Centralized Service Companies Under the Public Utility Holding Company Act of 2005, the Federal Power Act, and the Natural Gas Act, Final Rule published December 28, 2009 (RIN: 1902-AD86).

Contract Reporting Requirements of Intrastate Natural Gas Companies, Final Rule published May 26, 2010 (RIN: 1902-AD70).

[269] *Wholesale Competition in Regions With Organized Electric Markets*, Final Rule published October 28, 2008 (RIN: 1902-AD39).

Preventing Undue Discrimination and Preference in Transmission Service, Final Rule published March 15, 2007 (RIN: 1902-AD02).

Promotion of a More Efficient Capacity Release Market, Final Rule published June 30, 2008 (RIN: 1902-AD48).

[270] *Critical Energy Infrastructure Information*, Final Rule published November 14, 2007 (RIN: 1902-AD27).

[271] *Revisions to Form, Procedures, and Criteria for Certification of Qualifying Facility Status for a Small Power Production or Cogeneration Facility,* Final Rule published March 30, 2010 (RIN: 1902-AD92).

[272] *Mandatory Reliability Standards for Critical Infrastructure Protection,* Final Rule published February 7, 2008 (RIN: 1902-AD77).

[273] These included:
- Four rules that delegated or transferred an authority or function,
- Two procedural rules,
- Three rules updated annual filing fees with the Commission, based on the Commission's costs,
- Two rules updated project cost and annual limits for natural gas pipelines blanket construction certificates,
- A rule updating a Federal Reserve interest rate incorporated by reference, and
- A rule concerning FERC employee ethics.

[274] The SBA size standard for electric utilities is four million MWh per year. For gas companies it was $6.5 million in annual revenues in the earlier regulations and $7 million in the later regulations.

[275] That includes:
- Six rules that concerned mandatory electricity transmission reliability standards;
- Four rules that mandated adoption of consensus business practices standards,
- Three rules that affected posting, reporting, or filing requirements for natural gas companies,
- Three rules that were designed to increase the efficiency of energy markets, and
- One rule on critical infrastructure information.

[276] *Wholesale Competition in Regions With Organized Electric Markets* (RIN: 1902-AD39).

[277] Individual standards addressed:
- Critical Cyber Asset Identification,
- Security Management Controls,
- Personnel & Training,
- Electronic Security Perimeters,
- Physical Security of Critical Cyber Assets,
- Systems Security Management,
- Incident Reporting and Response Planning, and
- Recovery Plans for Critical Cyber Assets.

[278] The North American Electric Reliability Corporation (NERC) is the Commission-certified ERO.

[279] Registration thresholds included the following:
- "The ERO registers only those distribution providers or load serving entities that have a peak load of 25 MW or greater and are directly connected to the bulk electric system or are designated as a responsible entity as part of a required under-frequency load shedding program or a required under-voltage load shedding program."
- "The ERO registers only individual [generator] units of 20 MVA or greater that are directly connected to the bulk electric system [and] generating plants with an aggregate rating of 75 MVA or greater."

[280] One commenter estimated that this step reduced the number of power utilities subject to the Reliability Standard "from nearly 2,000 to approximately 326" (of which an estimated 296 were small).

[281] In the Information Collection Statement, the FERC tentatively estimated that municipal and cooperative utilities subject to all of the standards individually would incur a burden of 1,000 person-hours.

[282] *Federal Home Loan Bank Housing Associates, Core Mission Activities and Standby Letters of Credit*, Final Action published April 3, 2010 (RIN: 2590-AA33).

Federal Home Loan Bank Directors' Compensation and Expenses, Final Action published April 5, 2010 (RIN: 2590-AA31).

Board of Directors of Federal Home Loan Bank System Office of Finance, Final Action published May 3, 2010 (RIN: 2590-AA30).

Supplemental Standards of Ethical Conduct for Employees of the Federal Housing Finance Agency, Final Action published August 27, 2010 (RIN: 2590-AA02).

Federal Home Loan Bank Liabilities, Final Action published April 4, 2011 (RIN: 2590-AA36).

[283] *Portfolio Holdings*, Interim Final Rule published January 30, 2009; Final Action published December 28, 2010 (RIN: 2590-AA22).

Minimum Capital-Temporary Increase, Final Action published March 20, 2011 (RIN: 2590-AA01).

[284] *Reporting of Fraudulent Financial Instruments*, Final Action published January 27, 2010 (RIN: 2590-AA11). *Office of Ombudsman*, Final Action published February 10, 2011 (RIN: 2590-AA20).

Debt Collection Act, Final Action published March 20, 2011 (RIN: 2590-AA15).

2010 to 2011 Enterprise Affordable Housing Goals; Enterprise Book-Entry Procedures, Final Action published September 14, 2010 (RIN: 2590-AA26).

Equal Access to Justice Act Implementation, Final Action published October 22, 2010 (RIN: 2590-AA29). *Minority and Women Inclusion*, Final Action published December 28, 2010 (RIN: 2590-AA28).

[285] *Members of the Banks, Amendments — Community Development Financial Institutions Membership Eligibility*, Final Action published January 5, 2010 (RIN: 2590-AA18).

Affordable Housing Program Amendments: Federal Home Loan Bank Mortgage Refinancing Authority, Interim Final Rule published October 17, 2008; Second Interim Final Rule published August 8, 2009; Final Action published May 28, 2010 (RIN: 2590-AA04).

Use of Community Development Loans by CFIs To Secure Advances; Secured Lending by FHL Banks to Members and Their Affiliates; Transfer of Advances and New Business Activity Regulations, Final Action published December 9, 2010 (RIN: 2590-AA24).

Federal Home Loan Bank Housing Goals, Final Action published December 27, 2010 (RIN: 2590-AA16).

[286] *Federal Maritime Commission Reorganization*, Final Rule published May 26, 2010 (RIN: 3072-AC39).

[287] *Information Security Program*, Final Rule published February 24, 2011 (RIN: 3072-AC40).

[288] *Amendments to Commission's Rules of Practice and Procedure*, Final Rule published February 24, 2011 (RIN: 3072-AC41).

[289] *Repeal of Marine Terminal Agreement Exemption*, Final Action published December 10, 2009 (RIN: 3072- AC35). Commenters, including representatives of small business, shared these concerns and supported this action.

[290] *Port Restrictions and Requirements in the United States/Japan Trade*, Final Rule published March 4, 1997; Final Rule removed June 7, 1999; Requirement for reporting revised August 15, 2001; Reporting requirements terminated January 26, 2011 (RIN: 3072-AB97).

[291] This overview is based primarily on information from the Federal Reserve System website.

[292] *Regulation V: Fair Credit Reporting Risk-Based Pricing*, Final Rule published January 10, 2010 (RIM: 7100- AD22). This rule was issued jointly with the Federal Trade Commission.
Regulation Z: Truth in Lending Act Private Education Loans, Final Rule published August 14, 2009 (RIN: 7100-AD38).
Regulation Z: Truth in Lending Credit Card Fees and Interest Rate Changes, Final Rule published June 29, 2010. (RIN: 7100-AD36).
Regulation Z: Truth in Lending Credit Card Fees and Interest Rate Changes, Final Rule published June 29, 2010 (RIN: 7100-AD49).
Regulation Z: Truth in Lending Disclosures for Closed-end Mortgages, Final Rule published September 24, 2010 (RIN: 7100-AD33).
Regulation Z: Truth in Lending Consumer Notification of Mortgage Transfer, Final Rule published October 18, 2010 (RIN: 7100-AD46).
Regulation E: Electronic Funds Transfers, Final Rule published April 1, 2010; Final Rule published October 29, 2010 (RIN: 7100-AD47).

[293] *Regulation BB - Community Reinvestment Act*, Final Action published October 4, 2010 (RIN: 7100-AD39). Other agencies participating in this rulemaking included by the Federal Deposit Insurance Corporation (FDIC), the Office of the Comptroller of the Currency (Treasury), and the Office of Thrift Supervision (Treasury).
Regulation BB: Proposed Rule to Revise CRA Regulations to Support Activities Under the Neighborhood Stabilization Program, Final Rule published December 20, 2010 (RIN: 7100-AD50). Other agencies participating in this rulemaking included by the Federal Deposit Insurance Corporation (FDIC), the Office of the Comptroller of the Currency (Treasury), and the Office of Thrift Supervision (Treasury).

[294] *Regulation H and Y: Deduction of Goodwill Net of Associated Deferred Tax Liability*, Final Rule published December 30, 2008 (RIN: 7100-AD29). Other agencies participating in this rulemaking included the Federal Deposit Insurance Corporation (FDIC), the Office of the Comptroller of the Currency (Treasury), and the Office of Thrift Supervision (Treasury).
Regulation D: Reserve Requirements of Depository Institutions, Final Rule published October 28, 2010 (RIN: 7100-AD57).

[295] *Regulation E: Electronic Fund Transfers Overdraft Fee for ATM Withdrawals and One-time Card Transactions*, Final Rule published November 17, 2009 (RIN: 7100-AD27).

[296] *Regulation H--Registration of Mortgage Loan Originators*, Final Rule published July 28, 2010 (RIN: 7100- AD32). Other agencies participating in this rulemaking included the Federal Deposit Insurance Corporation (FDIC), the National Credit Union Administration (NCUA), the Farm Credit Administration (FCA), the Office of the Comptroller of the Currency (Treasury), and the Office of Thrift Supervision (Treasury).

[297] *Regulation H & Y: Risk-Based Capital Guidelines; Capital Adequacy Guidelines; Capital Maintenance; Capital—Residential Mortgage Loans Modified Pursuant to the Making Home Affordable Program*, Final Rule published December 21, 2009 (RIN: 7100-AD41). Other agencies participating in this rulemaking included by the Federal Deposit Insurance Corporation (FDIC), the Office of the Comptroller of the Currency (Treasury), and the Office of Thrift Supervision (Treasury).

[298] *Regulation Y: Conformance Period for Entities Engaged in Prohibited Proprietary Trading or Private Equity Fund or Hedge Fund Activities*, Final Rule published February 14, 2011 (RIN: 7100-AD58).

[299] *Regulation D: Reserve Requirements of Depository Institutions Policy on Payment System*, Final Rule published May 5, 2010 (RIN: 7100-AD48).

[300] *Regulation A: Extensions of Credit by Federal Reserve Banks*, Final Rule published December 12, 2009 (RIN: 7100-AD44).

[301] *Rules Regarding Access and Personal Information Under the Privacy Act of 1974*, Final Rule published October 18, 2010 (RIN: 7100-AD24).

[302] This included all seven disclosure/notification rules and all five rules issued under the Truth in Lending Act.

[303] This rule limited the ability of a financial institution to assess an overdraft fee for paying ATM withdrawals and one-time card transactions.

[304] This included both rules related to CRA consideration and the rule related to the HUD program.

[305] These included provision of term accounts and an option for handling deduction of goodwill.

[306] This rule set an eligibility requirement – registration with the SEC as a "nationally recognized statistical rating agency" – for providing credit ratings for the Term Asset-Backed Securities Loan Facility.

[307] This rule made an annual indexing adjustment for reserve requirements.

[308] This rule eased capital requirements and risk-weight requirements to encourage participation in a HUD program.

[309] The Paperwork Reduction Act estimated an average 40 hours for start-up and five hours per month for implementation. Since costs were mostly related to staff (training) or loan volume, they probably were roughly proportional to entity size and relatively small for smaller entities.

[310] In three rules the estimated number of affected small entities exceeded 10,000, and in a fourth it was unknown but probably even larger.

[311] For example: "The final rule implements new substantive requirements and updates to disclosure provisions in the Credit Card Act, which establishes fair and transparent practices relating to the extension of open-end consumer credit plans."

[312] For example: "It is desirable to expand eligibility for favorable CRA consideration to NSP-eligible areas and activities in order to provide financial institutions incentives to leverage NSP funding by providing loans, investments, and services in areas with high foreclosure or vacancy rates."

[313] In a disclosure rule on mortgages, for example, the number of small entities extending mortgage credit was estimated.

[314] "The Small Business Administration (SBA) has defined a small business as one whose annual receipts do not exceed $7 million or who have fewer than 500 employees. The Board expects that well over 90 percent of all businesses qualify as small businesses under the SBA's standards. Consequently a very large number of small entities could be subject to the final rules to the extent that they issue or sell gift certificates, store gift cards, or general-use prepaid cards."

[315] The Board estimated that mortgage credit was extended by approximately:

- 8,848 small depository institutions,
- 1,507 small non-depository institutions, and
- 17,041 mortgage brokers.

[316] This sort of situation characterized three rules certified as having no significant impact, four rules that the Board believed had no significant impact, and the two rules where an exemption from the RFA was claimed.

[317] "As a general matter, the Board's general risk-based capital rules apply only to a bank holding company that has consolidated assets of $500 million or more. Therefore, the changes to the

Board's capital adequacy guidelines for bank holding companies will not affect small bank holding companies."

[318] Regulation Z: Truth in Lending Disclosures for Closed-end Mortgages, *Response to the SBA* (75 FR 58531).

[319] PRA estimates are intended to be averages over the whole population of respondents and are thus generally inappropriate for regulatory flexibility analysis, but in a most rules the Board made no other cost estimates.

[320] This phenomenon occurs both when using industry-wide average data to assess impacts on small businesses and when using average data on all small businesses (by SBA standards) to assess impacts on very small businesses (e.g., smaller than the SBA standard by a factor of 5 or 10).

321 The exception applied to any employee "who has never been registered or licensed through the Registry as a mortgage loan originator if during the past 12 months the employee acted as a mortgage loan originator for 5 or fewer residential mortgage loans."

[322] For purposes of this rule, federal member banks were considered to be under FDIC jurisdiction.

[323] For comparison:
- The FDIC analysis made both distinctions,
- The NCUA did not estimate compliance costs,
- The FCA did not do a regulatory flexibility analysis on the grounds that the system is one large entity, and
- The two executive agencies (OCC and OTS) differentiated between entities subject to *de minimis* requirements and those subject to full requirements, but only in response to SBA comments.

[324] The Board's aggregate cost estimate worked out to $17,552 per small bank. By comparison:
- OCC's aggregate cost estimate was $18,600 per small national bank and $25,000 for full-requirement banks,
- OTS's aggregate cost estimate was $17,085 per small savings association and $17,441 for full-requirement savings associations, and
- FDIC's estimate for full-requirement banks was $17,379 for set-up and $7,436 annually.

[325] The OCC and OTS stated a standard of 5.0 percent of labor costs or 2.5 percent of non-interest expenses. The FDIC did not cite a standard estimate but estimated that first year full-requirement costs were less than 1 percent of revenue.

[326] This overview is based primarily on information from the FTC website.

[327] Three of the United Agenda listings contained multiple final rules, as the FTC gives the same RIN to similar rulemakings that stem from the same (recent) statute. Most of these final rules dated from the period 2003 through 2006, which was clearly outside the reference period. Three rules fell in the period 2007 through mid 2009. Those rules were not reviewed in detail because:
- Two final rules were joint rules with all the agencies that do financial regulation. These rules were early enough that they did not appear on any other agency's United Agenda listings from the target period. They regulated extremely diverse populations that were difficult to identify precisely. Moreover, such joint rules make the role of one agency difficult to discern.
- One final rule covered practices with affiliates. Because of their affiliations, the FTC doubted that any of the affected affiliated entities would qualify as "small." Small unaffiliated entities were not affected by the rule.

[328] *Trade Regulation Rule Relating to Power Output Claims for Amplifiers Utilized in Home Entertainment Products,* Confirmation of Rule published January 26, 2010 (RIN: 3084-AB09).

Rescission of Regulations Under the Comprehensive Smokeless Tobacco Health Education Act of 1986, Final Action published September 9, 2010 (RIN: 3084-AB23).

Appliance Labeling Rule (Light Bulbs), Final Rule published July 19, 2010 and April 12, 2011 (RIN: 3084-AB15). *Appliance Labeling Rule (Televisions),* Final Rule published January 6, 2011 (RIN: 3084-AB15).

Automotive Fuel Ratings, Certification, and Posting, Final Action published April 8, 2011 (RIN: 3084-AB14).

[329] *Free Annual File Disclosures,* Final Rule published March 3, 2010 (RIN: 3084-AA94).

Fair Credit Reporting Risk-Based Pricing Regulations, Final Rule published January 10, 2010 (RIN: 3084-AA94).

This rule was issued jointly with the Federal Reserve System.

Disclosures for Non-Federally Insured Depository Institutions Under the Federal Deposit Insurance Corporation Improvement Act, RIN: 3084-AA99. Final Action published June 4, 2010.

Mortgage Assistance Relief Services, Final Action published December 1, 2010 (RIN: 3084-AB18).

[330] *Privacy of Consumer Financial Information,* Final Action published December 1, 2009 (RIN: 3084-AA97). Other agencies participating in this rulemaking were the Federal Reserve System, the National Credit Union Administration (NCUA), the Federal Deposit Insurance Corporation (FDIC), the Commodity Futures Trading Commission (CTFC), the Securities and Exchange Commission (SEC), the Office of the Comptroller of the Currency (Treasury), and the Office of Thrift Supervision (Treasury).

[331] For one of the labeling requirements, for example, estimated costs to manufacturers were:
- Changing package and product labeling would result in one-time costs of:
    - $2,270 per manufacturer in labor costs,
    - $1,335 per product model for package label changes, and
    - $200 per product model for product labeling.
- Testing would result in one-time costs of $19.90 per product model.

Costs to catalog sellers were presumed to be quite small, as new catalogues have to be published periodically.

[332] A rule on disclosures for non-federally insured depository institutions under the Federal Deposit Insurance Corporation Improvement Act.

[333] A rule concerning risk-based pricing for credit offerings, for example:
- Offered several different ways that businesses can perform a risk-based pricing analysis, including:
    - Make individual, consumer-to-consumer comparisons,
    - Use the tiered pricing method to conduct the risk-based pricing analysis, and
    - Utilize a credit score notice; and
- Provided optional model notices and model credit score disclosures, which automatically qualified businesses for a safe harbor, to facilitate compliance.

[334] This overview is based primarily on information from the NCUA website.

[335] *Exception to the Maturity Limit on Second Mortgages,* Final Action published December 24, 2009 (RIN: 3133- AD64).

Short-Term, Small Amount Loans, Final Action published September 24, 2010 (RIN: 3133-AD71).

Secondary Capital Accounts, Final Action published September 23, 2010 (RIN: 3133-AD67).

[336] *National Credit Union Share Insurance Fund Premium and One Percent Deposit*, Final Action published November 19, 2009 (RIN: 3133-AD63).

Privacy of Consumer Financial Information, Final Action published December 1, 2009 (RIN: 3133-AC84). Other agencies participating in this rulemaking are the Office of the Comptroller of the Currency (OCC), the Federal Reserve System, the Federal Deposit Insurance Corporation (FDIC), the Office of Thrift Supervision (OTS), the Federal Trade Commission (FTC), the Commodity Futures Trading Commission (CTFC), and the Securities and Exchange Commission (SEC).

Chartering and Field of Membership for Federal Credit Unions, Final Action published June 25, 2010 (RIN: 3133-AD65).

Low-Income Definition, Final Action published December 23, 2010 (RIN: 3133-AD75).

Truth In Savings, Final Action published January 20, 2011 (RIN: 3133-AD72).

[337] *Corporate Credit Unions*, Final Action published October 20, 2010 (RIN: 3133-AD58).

Corporate Federal Credit Union Chartering Guidelines, Final Action published February 24, 2011 (RIN: 3133-AD80).

[338] *Display of Official Sign; Permanent Increase in Standard Maximum Share Insurance Amount*, Final Action published September 2, 2010 (RIN: 3133-AD78).

[339] *S.A.F.E. Mortgage Licensing Act*, Final Rule published July 28, 2010 (RIN: 3133-AD59). Other agencies participating in this rulemaking were the Federal Reserve System, the Federal Deposit Insurance Corporation (FDIC), the Federal Trade Commission (FTC), the Securities and Exchange Commission (SEC), the Commodity Futures Trading Commission (CFTC), and the Office of the Comptroller of the Currency (Treasury), the Office of Thrift Supervision (Treasury).

[340] *Fiduciary Duties at Federal Credit Unions; Mergers and Conversions of Insured Credit Unions*, Final Action published December 28, 2010 (RIN: 3133-AD40).

[341] *Unfair or Deceptive Acts or Practices; Clarifications*, Final Action published February 10, 2010 (RIN: 3133- AD62).

[342] *Fixed Assets, Member Business Loans, and Regulatory Flexibility Program*, Final Action published October 28, 2010 (RIN: 3133-AD68).

[343] NAICS 522110 (Commercial Banking); NAICS 522120 (Savings Institutions); NAICS 522130 (Credit Unions); and NAICS 522190 (Other Depository Credit Intermediation).

[344] About 98 percent of these are federally insured. In another rulemaking, the NCUA estimated that 3,168 federally-insured, state-chartered credit unions were small.

[345] In rulemakings on Deposit Insurance Fund assessments, by comparison, the FDIC reported that about 55 percent of financial institutions were small, but the size standard was 17.5 times the credit union standard.

[346] In some cases, the conclusion was stated without using the word "certify."

[347] In one of these rules the FDIC also referred to the analysis of the rule being clarified, which had shown no significant impacts; estimated that 692 credit unions would be affected; and provided a five-year phase-in period.

[348] This rule also had provisions concerning fiduciary responsibility and indemnification of individual credit union officials, but these did not affect credit unions as institutions.

[349] The NCUA "determined that this rule will not affect family well-being within the meaning of section 654 of the Treasury and General Government Appropriations Act."

[350] The exception applied to any employee "who has never been registered or licensed through the Registry as a mortgage loan originator if during the past 12 months the employee acted as a mortgage loan originator for 5 or fewer residential mortgage loans."

[351] As noted above, this was a regulation that the NCUA did not believe affected small credit unions.

[352] This overview is based primarily on information from the NGIC website.

[353] This overview is based primarily on information from the NLRB website.

[354] This overview is based primarily on information from the NRC website.

[355] *Miscellaneous Administrative Changes*, Final Rule published November 30, 2010 (RIN: 31950-AH49). *Administrative Changes: Clarification of the Location of Guidance for Electronic Submission and OtherMiscellaneous Corrections*, Final Rule published December 1, 2009 (RIN: 3150-AI73).

Nonprocurement Debarment and Suspension, Final Rule published May 19, 2010 (RIN: 3150-AI76).

NRC Region II Address and Main Telephone Number Changes, Final Rule published April 27, 2010 (RIN: 3150- AI80).

Public Records, Final Rule published July 16, 2010 (RIN: 3150-AI87).

[356] *Categorical Exclusions From Environmental Review*, Final Rule published April 19, 2010 (RIN: 31950-AI27).

[357] *List of Approved Spent Fuel Storage Casks: HI-STORM 100 Revision 7*, Final Rule published December 11, 2009 (RIN: 3150-AI71).

List of Approved Spent Fuel Storage Casks: MAGNASTOR System, Revision 1, Final Rule published June 16, 2010 (RIN: 3150-AI86).

List of Approved Spent Fuel Storage Casks: NAC-MPC System, Revision 6, Final Rule published July 21, 2010 (RIN: 3150-AI88).

Consideration of Environmental Impacts of Temporary Storage of Spent Fuel After Cessation of Reactor Operation, Final Rule published December 23, 2010 (RIN: 31950-AI47.

List of Approved Spent Fuel Storage Casks: NUHOMS® HD System, Revision 1, Final Rule published January 13, 2011 (RIN: 3150-AI89).

[358] *Alternate Fracture Toughness Requirements for Protection Against Pressurized Thermal Shock Events*, Final
Rule published January 4, 2010 (RIN: 31950-AI01).

Increase in the Primary Nuclear Liability Insurance Premium, Final Rule published April 2, 2010 (RIN: 3150-AI74).

Domestic Licensing of Production and Utilization Facilities; Updates to Incorporation by Reference of Regulatory Guide, Final Rule published October 5, 2010 (RIN: 31950-AI37).

[359] *Export and Import of Nuclear Equipment and Materials; Updates and Clarifications*, Final Rule published July 28, 2010 (RIN: 31950-AI16).

License and Certificate of Compliance Terms, Final Rule published February 16, 2011 (RIN: 31950-AI09).

[360] *Revision of Fee Schedules; Fee Recovery for FY 2010*, Final Rule published December 23, 2010 (RIN: 31950- AI70).

[361] A firm in NAICS 221113 (Nuclear Electric Power Generation) "is small if, including its affiliates, it is primarily engaged in the generation, transmission, and/or distribution of electric energy for sale and its total electric output for the preceding fiscal year did not exceed 4 million megawatt hours."

[362] "A small business is a for-profit concern and is a --

(1) Concern that provides a service or a concern not engaged in manufacturing with average gross receipts of $6.5 million or less over its last 3 completed fiscal years; or

(2) Manufacturing concern with an average number of 500 or fewer employees based upon employment during each pay period for the preceding 12 calendar months."

These size standards are much the same as the size standards most widely used by the SBA throughout industry. More general standards are necessary because some entities regulated by the NRC are outside the electric power industry.

[363] A NPRM was published, so that exemption from the NPRM notice and comment requirements was not claimed, but otherwise the rule read rather like an internal agency matter.

[364] Licensees under 10 CFR part 171, which include power reactors, non-power reactors, spent fuel storage/reactor decommissioning, transportation, uranium recovery, and materials users.

[365] Originally, the statute required NRC to recover through fees 100 percent of its budget authority - not including amounts appropriated from the Nuclear Waste Fund (NWF), amounts appropriated for Waste Incidental to Reprocessing (WIR), and amounts appropriated for generic homeland security activities. Prior to this rule, the recovery level was reduced to 90 percent.

[366] This category currently includes:

- Manufacturing entities with fewer than 35 employees,
- Other businesses and non-profit organizations with annual gross receipts of less than $450,000,
- Governmental jurisdictions with a population less than 20,000, and
- Educational institutions that are not publicly supported that have fewer than 35 employees.

[367] This overview is based primarily on information from the OSHRC website.

[368] This overview is based primarily on information from the PRC website.

[369] *Periodic Reporting of Service Performance Measurements and Customer Satisfaction,* Final Action Notice published July 6 2010 (RIN: 3211-AA05).

[370] *Periodic Reporting Exceptions,* Final Action Notice published September 23, 2010 (RIN: 3211-AA06).

[371] This overview is based primarily on information from the RATB website.

[372] *Implementation of the Privacy Act of 1974,* Final Action Notice published November 20, 2009 (RIN: 0430-AA00). *Privacy Act Regulations,* Final Action Notice published June 29, 2010 (RIN: 0430-AA03).

[373] *Rule Implementing the Freedom of Information Act,* Final Action Notice published November 20, 2009 (RIN: 0430-AA01).

[374] This overview is based primarily on information from the SEC website.

[375] The various stock exchanges, such as the New York Stock Exchange, and American Stock Exchange are SROs. The Financial Industry Regulatory Authority, which operates the NASDAQ system, is also an SRO.

[376] *Amendments to Form ADV,* Final Action published August 12, 2010 (RIN: 3235-AI17). *Amendment to Municipal Securities Disclosure,* Final Action published June 1, 2010 (RIN: 3235-AJ66). *Disclosure for Asset-Backed Securities Required by Section 943 of the Dodd-Frank Wall Street Reform and Consumer Protection Act,* Final Action published January 26, 2011 (RIN: 3235-AK75).

[377] *Proxy Solicitation Enhancements,* Final Action published December 23, 2009 (RIN: 3235-AK28).

[378] *Rules for Nationally Recognized Statistical Rating Organizations*, Final Action published December 12, 2009 (RIN: 3235-AK14).

[379] *Custody of Funds or Securities of Clients by Investment Advisers*, Final Action published January 11, 2010 (RIN: 3235-AK32).

Amendments to Regulation SHO, Final Action published March 10, 2010 (RIN: 3235-AK35).

Political Contributions by Certain Investment Advisers, Final Action published July 14, 2010 (RIN: 3235-AK39). *Management Controls for Brokers or Dealers With Market Access*, Final Action published November 15, 2010 (RIN: 3235-AK53).

Temporary Rule Regarding Principal Trades With Certain Advisory Clients, Final Action published December 30, 2010 (RIN: 3235-AJ96).

[380] *Extension of Filing Accommodation for Static Pool Information in Filings With Respect to Asset-Backed Securities*, Final Action published December 21, 2009 (RIN: 3235-AK44); Final Action published December 22, 2010 (RIN: 3235-AK70).

Money Market Funds, Final Action published March 4, 2010 (RIN: 3235-AK33).

Interim Rule for Reporting Pre-Enactment Security-Based Swap Transactions, Interim Final Rule published October 20, 2010 (RIN: 3235-AK73).

[381] *Transitional Registration as a Municipal Advisor*, Interim Final Rule published September 8, 2010 (RIN: 3235- AK69).

Issuer Review of Assets in Offerings of Asset-Backed Securities, Final Action published January 25, 2011 (RIN: 3235-AK76).

[382] *Facilitating Shareholder Director Nominations*, Final Action published September 16, 2010 (RIN: 3235-AK27). *Shareholder Approval of Executive Compensation and Golden Parachute Compensation,* Final Action published February 2, 2011 (RIN: 3235-AK68).

[383] *Model Privacy Form Under the Gramm-Leach-Bliley Act*, Final Action published December 1, 2009 (RIN: 3235-AJ06). The other agencies participating in this rulemaking were the Office of the Comptroller of the Currency (OCC), the Federal Reserve System, the Federal Deposit Insurance Corporation (FDIC), the National Credit Union Administration (NCUA), the Office of Thrift Supervision (OTS), the Federal Trade Commission (FTC), and the Commodity Futures Trading Commission (CFTC).

[384] *References to Ratings of Nationally Recognized Statistical Rating Organizations*, Final Action published October 9, 2009 (RIN: 3235-AK17; RIN: 3235-AK19).

[385] *Amendments to Rules Requiring Internet Availability of Proxy Materials*, Final Action published February 27, 2010 (RIN: 3235-AK25).

[386] *Temporary Exemptions for Eligible Credit Default Swaps To Facilitate Operation of Central Counterparties To Clear and Settle Credit Default Swaps*, Interim Final Rule published January 22, 2009; extended September 17, 2009 and November 26, 2010. (RIN: 3235-AK26).

[387] *Amendments to the Informal and Other Procedures, Rules of Organization and Program Management, and Rules of Practice; Interim Commission Review of Public Company Accounting Oversight Board*, Final Action published August 6, 2010 (RIN: 3235-AJ34).

[388] NAICS 523 (Financial Investments and Related Activities); NAICS 524 (Insurance Carriers and Related Activities – except Direct Property and Casualty Insurance Carriers, for which it is 1,500 employees); and NAICS 525 (Funds, Trusts and Other Financial Vehicles).

[389] This definition is applied to businesses in general (where needed), to NRSROs, and to alternative trading systems, which must register as broker-dealers.

[390] 17 CFR 240.0-10(a) (Securities Exchange Act) and 17 CFR 230.157 (Securities Act)

[391] 17 CFR 240.0-10(c) (Securities Exchange Act)

[392] 17 CFR 240.0-10(f) (Securities Exchange Act)

[393] 17 CFR 240.0-10(e) (Securities Exchange Act)

[394] 17 CFR 270.0-10 (Investment Company Act)

[395] 17 CFR 275.0-10 (Investment Advisors Act)

[396] 17 CFR 240.0-10(d) (Securities Exchange Act)

[397] Estimates vary in part because they were based on data at different points in time.

[398] In the rule for a model privacy form under the Gramm-Leach-Bliley Act, for example, "the SEC estimate[d] that 915 broker-dealers, 212 investment companies registered with the Commission, and 781 investment advisers registered with the Commission are small entities for purposes of the RFA.

[399] The SEC noted that "a delayed compliance date for smaller reporting companies

- will allow those companies to observe how the rule operates for other companies and may allow them to better prepare for the implementation of the rules, and...
- will give the [SEC] a further opportunity to consider adjustments for smaller reporting companies."

[400] For example, although the provisions were not limited to small businesses, the SEC noted in one rule:

- "The amendments clarify when an investment adviser, including a small adviser, has custody."
- "We are providing updated guidance for accountants that modernize the procedures for the surprise examination and should provide clarification to investment advisers, including small entities, and accountants on certain issues regarding the surprise examination."

[401] For example, "based on our past experience, we believe the amendments will be more useful to investors if there are specific disclosure requirements... In addition, the specific disclosure requirements in the amendments will promote consistent and comparable disclosure among all companies."

[402] *Solid Waste Rail Transfer Facilities*, Interim Final Rule published January 27, 2009. Correction published December 22, 2009 (RIN: 2140-AA92).

[403] *Annual Submission of Tax Information for Use in the Revenue Shortfall Allocation Method*, Final Action Notice published February 26, 2010 (RIN: 2140-AA98).

[404] A governor of a state may petition the STB to require that a facility obtain a land-use-exemption permit.

[405] Two Canadian and two Mexican rail carriers were also affected.

In: Independent Federal Agency Compliance ...   ISBN: 978-1-62948-195-1
Editors: L. Jarvis and B. Leighton   © 2013 Nova Science Publishers, Inc.

Chapter 2

THE RFA IN A NUTSHELL: A CONDENSED GUIDE TO THE REGULATORY FLEXIBILITY ACT[*]

Small Business Administration, Office of Advocacy

FOREWORD

When government takes small businesses into consideration in developing regulations, it saves time and money for a vital sector of the nation's economy, our small businesses.

This primer on the Regulatory Flexibility Act (RFA) is designed to be used by those interested in the basics of federal regulatory compliance with respect to the RFA and Executive Order 13272. For more detailed guidance on the RFA, federal agency rule writers and policy analysts should refer to the Office of Advocacy's step-by-step manual: *A Guide for Government Agencies: How to Comply with the Regulatory Flexibility Act* (www.sba.gov/ advo/laws/rfaguide.pdf).

The chief counsel for advocacy of the U.S. Small Business Administration has been designated to monitor agency compliance with the Regulatory Flexibility Act.

---

[*] This is an edited, reformatted and augmented version of a Small Business Administration, Office of Advocacy publication, dated October 2010.

INTRODUCTION TO THE RFA

The Regulatory Flexibility Act (RFA), enacted in September 1980,[1] requires agencies to consider the impact of their regulatory proposals on small entities, to analyze effective alternatives that minimize small entity impacts, and to make their analyses available for public comment. The RFA applies to three types of small entities:

- *Small Businesses:* Defined by section 3 of the Small Business Act.[2]
- *Small Nonprofits:* Any nonprofit enterprise that is independently owned and operated and not dominant in its field.
- *Small Governmental Jurisdictions:* Governments of cities, counties, towns, townships, villages, school districts, or special districts with a population of less than 50,000.

The RFA does not seek preferential treatment for small entities, require agencies to adopt regulations that impose the least burden on small entities, or mandate exemptions for small entities. Rather, it requires agencies to examine public policy issues using an analytical process that identifies, among other things, barriers to small business competitiveness and seeks a level playing field for small entities, not an unfair advantage.

In essence, the RFA asks agencies to be aware of the economic structure of the entities they regulate and the effect their regulations may have on small entities. It requires agencies to analyze the economic impact of proposed regulations when there is likely to be a significant economic impact on a substantial number of small entities, and to consider regulatory alternatives that will achieve the agency's goal while minimizing the burden on small entities.

The Small Business Regulatory Enforcement Fairness Act (SBREFA), enacted in March 1996,[3] amended the RFA and provided additional tools to aid small businesses in the fight for regulatory fairness. The most significant amendments made by SBREFA were:

- Judicial review of agency compliance with some of the RFA's provisions.
- Requirements for more detailed and substantive regulatory flexibility analyses.

- Expanded participation by small entities in the development of rules by the Occupational Safety and Health Administration (OSHA) and the Environmental Protection Agency (EPA).

The goal of Congress in creating the RFA was to change the regulatory culture in agencies and mandate that they consider regulatory alternatives that achieve statutory purposes, while still minimizing the impacts on small entities. Regulatory flexibility analyses built into the regulatory development process at the earliest stages will help agency decision makers achieve regulatory goals with realistic, cost-effective, and less burdensome regulations.

This primer should be utilized by anyone interested in commenting on draft federal regulations on behalf of small business and as a short description of the basic requirements of the act.

FIRST STEPS: WHERE DO WE BEGIN?

If you had to break down the RFA into sections, there are really four main parts. It's easiest to think of them as four related questions:

- Does the RFA apply to this rule?
- Will this rule have a significant economic impact on a substantial number of small entities?
- What is the potential economic impact of the rule on small entities?
- What has been done to minimize the adverse economic impact of the rule on small entities that was described in the proposed rule?

The following sections explain how to answer those important questions.

DOES THE RFA APPLY?

One of the first decisions to make is whether the Regulatory Flexibility Act applies to a particular regulation. The RFA applies to any rule subject to notice and comment rulemaking under section 553(b) of the Administrative Procedure Act (APA)[4] or any other law. However there are times when a regulation or rule can be exempt from the APA notice and comment requirements, thereby exempting it from the RFA as well. Rules are exempt when any of the following is involved: (1) a military or foreign affairs function of the United States, or (2) a matter relating to agency management or personnel or to public property, loans, grants, benefits, or contracts.[5] In addition, except where notice or hearing is required by statute, the APA does not apply (1) to interpretative rules, general statements of policy, or rules of agency organization, procedure or practice; or (2) when the agency for good cause finds that notice and public procedure are impracticable, unnecessary, or contrary to the public interest.[6]

The RFA presents its own exemptions as well. Section 601(2) states that the RFA does not apply to rules of particular applicability relating to rates, wages, corporate or financial structures, or reorganizations thereof, prices, facilities, appliances, services or allowances.[7]

CAN YOU CERTIFY? THE THRESHOLD ANALYSIS

Once an agency determines that the RFA applies to their draft rule, it must decide whether to conduct a full regulatory flexibility analysis or to certify that the proposed rule will not "have a significant economic impact on a substantial number of small entities."[8]

In order to certify a rule under the RFA, an agency should be able to answer the following types of questions:

- Which small entities will be affected?
- Have adequate economic data been obtained?
- What are the economic implications/impacts of the proposal and do the data reveal a significant economic impact on a substantial number of small entities?

If, after conducting an analysis for a proposed or final rule, an agency determines that a rule will not have a significant economic impact on a substantial number of small entities, section 605(b) of the RFA provides that the head of the agency may certify, or promise, that the rule will not have this effect. The certification must include a statement providing the *factual* basis for this determination, and the certification must be published in the *Federal Register* at the time the proposed or final rule is published for public comment. A certification must include, at a minimum, a description of the affected entities and an estimate of the cost of the impacts that clearly justifies the "no impact" certification. The agency's reasoning and assumptions underlying its certification should be explicit in order to obtain public comment and thus receive information that would be used to re-evaluate the certification. Clearly, an agency should identify the scope of the problem and the impact of the solution on affected entities before moving forward with a regulatory proposal.

DEVELOPING THE THRESHOLD ANALYSIS

Certification analysis does not require the depth of analysis necessary in an initial regulatory flexibility analysis. Nevertheless, this "threshold" analysis can offer important insights into the nature of regulatory impacts.

The Office of Advocacy believes the threshold analysis should include the following items in order to support an adequate certification statement:

1) Description of small entities affected
   - A brief economic and technical statement on the regulated community, describing some of the following types of information:
     a) The diversity in size of regulated entities
     b) Revenues in each size grouping
2) Economic impacts on small entities.
   - A fair, first estimate of expected cost impacts, or a reasonable basis for assuming costs would be insignificant within all economic or size groupings of the "small" regulated community.
   - The rationale for the certification decision, based on the analysis presented.
3) Significant economic impact criteria.
   - The criteria used to examine whether first-estimate costs are significant.
4) Substantial number criteria.
   - The criteria used to examine whether the entities experiencing significant impacts constitute a substantial number of entities in any of the regulated size groupings.
5) Description of assumptions and uncertainties.
   - The sources of data used in the economic and technical analysis.
   - The degree of uncertainty in the cost estimates, when uncertainty is large.

After the 1996 amendment, the RFA now requires that certifications be supported by a "statement of factual basis." In amending the RFA, Congress intended that agencies should do more than provide boilerplate and unsubstantiated statements to support their RFA certifications. Courts will overturn an agency's final certification if it is not adequate.[9] Consequently, certifications that simply state that the agency has found that the proposed or final rule will not have a significant economic impact on a substantial number of small entities are not sufficient under section 605(b) of the RFA.

Definition of "Significant" and "Substantial"

A critical decision point in the threshold analysis is for the agency to determine whether there is a significant economic impact on a substantial number of small entities. The RFA does not define "significant" or "substantial." What is "significant" or "substantial" will vary depending on the problem that needs to be addressed, the rule's requirements, and the preliminary assessment of the rule's impact. The agency is in the best position to gauge the small entity impacts of its regulations.

Direct versus Indirect Impact

The courts have held that the RFA requires an agency to perform a regulatory flexibility analysis of small entity impacts only when a rule directly regulates them. Although it is not required by the RFA, the Office of Advocacy believes that it is good public policy for the agency to perform a regulatory flexibility analysis even when the impacts of its regulation are indirect. If an agency can accomplish its statutory mission in a more cost-effective manner, the Office of Advocacy believes that it is good public policy to do so.

WHEN MORE IN-DEPTH ANALYSIS IS REQUIRED: THE IRFA

During the preparation of a proposed rule, an agency must prepare an initial regulatory flexibility analysis (IRFA) if it determines that a proposal may impose a significant economic impact on a substantial number of small entities. The RFA requires agencies to publish the IRFA, or a summary, in the *Federal Register* at the same time it publishes the proposed rulemaking.[10] The IRFA must include a discussion of each element required by section 603 of the RFA, and the agency must also send a copy of the IRFA to the Chief Counsel for Advocacy.[11] Executive Order 13272 requires agencies to notify Advocacy when the agency submits a draft proposed or final rule to the Office of Information and Regulatory Affairs (OIRA) under Executive Order 12866, or at a reasonable time prior to publication of the rule by the agency.[12]

Questions to Consider

Section 603 of the RFA requires agencies to perform a detailed analysis of the potential impact of the proposed rule on small entities.[13] Some of the important questions the agency should address in preparing an IRFA are:

- Which small entities are affected the most? Are all small entities in an industry affected equally or do some experience disparate impacts such that aggregation of the industry data would dilute the magnitude of the economic effect on specific subgroups?
- Are all the required elements of an IRFA present, including a clear explanation of the need for and objectives of the rule?
- Has the agency identified and analyzed all major cost factors?
- Has the agency identified all significant alternatives that would allow the agency to accomplish its regulatory objectives while minimizing the adverse impact or maximizing the benefits to small entities?
- Can the agency use other statutorily required analyses to supplement or satisfy the IRFA requirements of the RFA?
- Are there circumstances under which preparation of an IRFA may be waived or delayed?
- What portion of the problem is attributable to small businesses (i.e., is regulation of small businesses needed to satisfy the statutory objectives)?
- Does the proposed solution meet the statutory objectives in a more cost-effective or cost-beneficial manner than any of the alternatives considered?

The preparation of an IRFA should be coordinated with the development of the data and analysis the agency will use in preparing the proposed rule under the requirements of the Administrative Procedure Act. In doing so, the agency should be mindful of the requirements of the RFA and collect data based on size. The development of a rational rule will require the acquisition of data that describe the scope of the problem, the entities affected, and the extent of those effects. Without such information, the agency will be unable to develop a rational rule. When data are not readily available, the agency should consult with industry sources or other third parties to collect data. If the data collection is inadequate, then agencies should solicit the data as part of the proposed rulemaking. [14]

Elements of an IRFA

Under section 603(b) of the RFA, an IRFA must describe the impact of the proposed rule on small entities and contain the following information:

1) A description of the reasons why the action by the agency is being considered.
2) A succinct statement of the objectives of, and legal basis for, the proposed rule.
3) A description—and, where feasible, an estimate of the number—of small entities to which the proposed rule will apply.
4) A description of the projected reporting, recordkeeping, and other compliance requirements of the proposed rule, including an estimate of the classes of small entities that will be subject to the requirement and the types of professional skills necessary for preparation of the report or record.
5) An identification, to the extent practicable, of all relevant federal rules that may duplicate, overlap, or conflict with the proposed rule.
6) A description of any significant alternatives to the proposed rule which accomplish the stated objectives of applicable statues and which minimize any significant economic impact of the proposed rule on small entities.

The principal issues an agency should address in an IRFA are the impact of a proposed rule on small entities and the comparative effectiveness and costs of alternative regulatory options.

Significant Alternatives are the Key

The keystone of the IRFA is the description of any significant alternatives to the proposed rule that accomplish the stated objectives of applicable statutes and that minimize the rule's economic impact on small entities. It is the development and adoption of these alternatives that provide regulatory relief to small entities.

Analyzing alternatives establishes a process for the agency to evaluate proposals that achieve the regulatory goals efficiently and effectively without unduly burdening small entities, erecting barriers to competition, or stifling innovation. This process provides an additional filter by which the agency conducts rational rulemaking mandated by the APA.

Rather than focus on the overall costs and benefits of a particular regulation (as might be required by statute, such as the best achievable control technology, or by the regulatory analysis requirements of E.O. 12866), the RFA requires the agency to undertake an analysis that determines the impacts of the rule on small entities and then considers alternatives that reduce or minimize those impacts. Instead of analyzing the impacts of its regulatory actions on all relevant sectors of the economy, the IRFA narrows the scope of the particular review to small entities. The premise underpinning the IRFA is that, everything else being equal, the most rational alternative is often the one that achieves the objective of the agency at the lowest cost. Since small entities often have the highest costs to comply with a rule, while contributing the least to the problem the rule addresses, it makes sense to analyze them separately from all other regulated entities to determine if the rule can be made more cost effective by employing alternative standards for small entities.

The kinds of alternatives that are possible will vary based on the particular regulatory objective and the characteristics of the regulated industry. However, section 603(c) of the RFA gives agencies some alternatives that they must consider, at a minimum:

- Establishment of different compliance or reporting requirements for small entities or timetables that take into account the resources available to small entities.
- Clarification, consolidation, or simplification of compliance and reporting requirements for small entities.
- Use of performance rather than design standards.

- Exemption for certain or all small entities from coverage of the rule, in whole or in part.

Additional alternatives include adopting different standards based on the sizes of businesses or modifying the types of equipment required for large and small entities. In short, the agency should consider a variety of mechanisms to reach the regulatory objective.

Consistent with an agency's obligations under section 609 of the RFA, agencies should perform outreach to interested groups to help develop regulatory solutions. In doing so, agency personnel should recognize that different sectors of an industry may have very different perspectives on a particular regulatory approach. The agency, before adopting one approach, should ensure that it contacts small entities and their representatives as well as large entities and their representatives. This type of communication is not prohibited by the APA and will help the agency focus on potential benefits and costs of various approaches to small businesses.

THE FINAL RULE STAGE: THE FRFA

When it comes time to draft the final rule, the RFA requires agencies to either publish a certification statement with a factual basis as in the proposed rule, or a final regulatory flexibility analysis (FRFA). Agencies must prepare a FRFA unless the agency finds that the final rule will not have a significant economic impact on a substantial number of small entities or the final rule is issued under the APA provision allowing for good cause to forego notice and comment rulemaking.

The RFA mandates that agencies revise their initial regulatory flexibility analysis based on the public comments received. Agencies routinely create a summary of the public's comments to be published along with the final rules. In developing this summary, the agency should specifically summarize comments from small entities. Once the agency determines that it cannot certify the final rule under section 605(b), the agency must prepare a FRFA. If the agency determines that the rulemaking will not result in a significant economic impact on a substantial number of small entities, the head of the agency may so certify under section 605(b) of the RFA, and provide a copy of the certification to the Chief Counsel for Advocacy.

Questions to Consider

A number of important questions will assist the agency in preparing a final regulatory flexibility analysis under the RFA:

- Have all significant issues raised in the public comments regarding the IRFA been summarized and assessed and have any changes been made to the rule as a result of those comments?
- Has the number of small entities been estimated? If not, did the agency explain why?
- Has the adverse economic impact on small entities been minimized?
- Have all significant alternatives been reviewed?

Elements of a FRFA

Section 604(a) of the RFA outlines the central issues the agency must address in the FRFA. In short, agencies must evaluate the impact of a rule on small entities and describe their efforts to minimize the adverse impact. Agencies are required to publish a small entity compliance guide whenever they publish a rule that contains a FRFA. This must be done at the same time the final rule is published in the *Federal Register.*

The requirements, outlined in section 604(a)(1)–(5), are highlighted in italics below:

1) *A succinct statement of the need for, and objectives of, the rule.* The agency can cross-reference to a similar succinct statement in the supplementary information if the cross reference enables small entities to easily identify the need for and objectives of the rule.
2) *A summary of the significant issues raised by the public comments in response to the IRFA, a summary of the assessment of the agency of such issues, and a statement of any changes made in the proposed rule as a result of such comments.* Under the APA, agencies are required to respond to comments addressing relevant statutory considerations. Since the RFA constitutes a relevant statutory consideration, the agency is obligated under the APA to respond to comments on the RFA and relate how it changed the proposal, if at all, in response to the comments.

3) *A description and an estimate of the number of small entities to which the rule will apply or an explanation of why no such estimate is available.*

4) *A description of the projected reporting, recordkeeping, and other compliance requirements of the rule, including an estimate of the classes of small entities that will be subject to the requirement and the types of professional skills necessary for preparation of the report or record.*

5) *A description of the steps the agency has taken to minimize the significant adverse economic impact on small entities consistent with the stated objectives of applicable statutes, including a statement of the factual, policy, and legal reasons for selecting the alternative adopted in the final rule and why each of the other significant alternatives to the rule considered by the agency was rejected.*

A WORD ON REGULATORY PANELS

In 1996, SBREFA amended the RFA to include a number of important provisions. One of those was section 609, which requires, among other things, that certain agencies conduct special outreach efforts to ensure that small entity views are carefully considered prior to the issuance of a proposed rule. This outreach is accomplished through the work of small business advocacy review panels, often referred to as SBREFA panels.

WHO MUST HOLD SBREFA PANELS?

The statute requires that the Environmental Protection Agency (EPA), the Occupational Safety and Health Administration (OSHA) and the Consumer Finance Protection Bureau (CFPB) evaluate their regulatory proposals to determine whether SBREFA panels should be convened.

CONCLUSION

The RFA does not seek preferential treatment for small entities, does not require agencies to adopt regulations that impose the least burden on small entities, and does not mandate exemptions for small entities. Rather, as this guide has illustrated, the RFA establishes an analytical process for determining how public policy issues can best be achieved without erecting barriers to competition, stifling innovation, or imposing undue burdens on small entities. In so doing, it seeks a level playing field for small entities.

APPENDIX A: THE REGULATORY FLEXIBILITY ACT

The following text of the Regulatory Flexibility Act of 1980, as amended, is taken from Title 5 of the United States Code, sections 601–612. The Regulatory Flexibility Act was originally passed in 1980 (P.L. 96-354). The act was amended by the Small Business Regulatory Enforcement Fairness Act of 1996 (P.L. 104-121) and the Dodd-Frank Wall Street Reform and Consumer Protection Act of 2010 (P.L. 11-203)

Congressional Findings and Declaration of Purpose

(a) The Congress finds and declares that —
1) when adopting regulations to protect the health, safety and economic welfare of the Nation, Federal agencies should seek to achieve statutory goals as effectively and efficiently as possible without imposing unnecessary burdens on the public;
2) laws and regulations designed for application to large scale entities have been applied uniformly to small businesses, small organizations, and small governmental jurisdictions even though the problems that gave rise to government action may not have been caused by those smaller entities;
3) uniform Federal regulatory and reporting requirements have in numerous instances imposed unnecessary and disproportionately burdensome demands including legal, accounting and consulting costs upon small businesses, small organizations, and small governmental jurisdictions with limited resources;
4) the failure to recognize differences in the scale and resources of regulated entities has in numerous instances adversely affected competition in the marketplace, discouraged innovation and restricted improvements in productivity;

5) unnecessary regulations create entry barriers in many industries and discourage potential entrepreneurs from introducing beneficial products and processes;

6) the practice of treating all regulated businesses, organizations, and governmental jurisdictions as equivalent may lead to inefficient use of regulatory agency resources, enforcement problems and, in some cases, to actions inconsistent with the legislative intent of health, safety, environmental and economic welfare legislation;

7) alternative regulatory approaches which do not conflict with the stated objectives of applicable statutes may be available which minimizethe significant economic impact of rules on small businesses, small organizations, and small governmental jurisdictions;

8) the process by which Federal regulations are developed and adopted should be reformed to require agencies to solicit the ideas and comments of small businesses, small organizations, and small governmental jurisdictions to examine the impact of proposed and existing rules on such entities, and to review the continued need for existing rules.

9) It is the purpose of this Act [enacting this chapter and provisions set out as notes under this section] to establish as a principle of regulatory issuance that agencies shall endeavor, consistent with the objectives of the rule and of applicable statutes, to fit regulatory and informational requirements to the scale of the businesses, organizations, and governmental jurisdictions subject to regulation. To achieve this principle, agencies are required to solicit and consider flexible regulatory proposals and to explain the rationale for their actions to assure that such proposals are given serious consideration.

REGULATORY FLEXIBILITY ACT[15]

Sections

SEC. 601. Definitions [Cite: 5 USC 01]

For purposes of this chapter—

(1) the term "agency" means an agency as defined in section 551(1) of this title;

(2) the term "rule" means any rule for which the agency publishes a general notice of proposed rulemaking pursuant to section 553(b) of this title, or any other law, including any rule of general applicability governing Federal grants to State and local governments for which the agency provides an opportunity for notice and public comment, except that the term "rule" does not include a rule of particular applicability relating to rates, wages, corporate or financial structures or reorganizations thereof, prices, facilities, appliances, services, or allowances therefor or to valuations, costs or accounting, or practices relating to such rates, wages, structures, prices, appliances, services, or allowances;

(3) the term "small business" has the same meaning as the term "small business concern" under section 3 of the Small Business Act, unless an agency, after consultation with the Office of Advocacy of the Small Business Administration and after opportunity for public comment, establishes one or more definitions of such term which are appropriate to the activities of the agency and publishes such definition(s) in the *Federal Register*;

(4) the term "small organization" means any not-for-profit enterprise which is independently owned and operated and is not dominant in its field, unless an agency establishes, after opportunity for public comment, one or more definitions of such term which are appropriate

to the activities of the agency and publishes such definition(s) in the *Federal Register*;

(5) the term "small governmental jurisdiction" means governments of cities, counties, towns, townships, villages, school districts, or special districts, with a population of less than fifty thousand, unless an agency establishes, after opportunity for public comment, one or more definitions of such term which are appropriate to the activities of the agency and which are based on such factors as location in rural or sparsely populated areas or limited revenues due to the population of such jurisdiction, and publishes such definition(s) in the *Federal Register*;

(6) the term "small entity" shall have the same meaning as the terms "small business", "small organization" and "small governmental jurisdiction" defined in paragraphs (3), (4) and (5) of this section; and

(7) the term "collection of information"—

A. means the obtaining, causing to be obtained, soliciting, or requiring the disclosure to third parties or the public, of facts or opinions by or for an agency, regardless of form or format, calling for either—

i. answers to identical questions posed to, or identical reporting or recordkeeping requirements imposed on, 10 or more persons, other than agencies, instrumentalities, or employees of the United States; or

ii. answers to questions posed to agencies, instrumentalities, or employees of the United States which are to be used for general statistical purposes; and

B. shall not include a collection of information described under section 3518(c)(1) of title 44, United States Code.

(8) recordkeeping requirement.—The term "recordkeeping requirement" means a requirement imposed by an agency on persons to maintain specified records.

(Added Pub. L. 96-354, Sec. 3(a), Sept. 19, 1980, 94 Stat. 1165; amended Pub. L. 104- 121, title II, Sec. 241(a)(2), Mar. 29, 1996, 110 Stat. 864.)

SEC. 602. Regulatory Agenda [Cite: 5 USC 602]

a) During the months of October and April of each year, each agency shall publish in the *Federal Register* a regulatory flexibility agenda which shall contain—

   (1) a brief description of the subject area of any rule which the agency expects to propose or promulgate which is likely to have a significant economic impact on a substantial number of small entities;

   (2) a summary of the nature of any such rule under consideration for each subject area listed in the agenda pursuant to paragraph (1), the objectives and legal basis for the issuance of the rule, and an approximate schedule for completing action on any rule for which the agency has issued a general notice of proposed rulemaking; and

   (3) the name and telephone number of an agency official knowledgeable concerning the items listed in paragraph (1).

b) Each regulatory flexibility agenda shall be transmitted to the Chief Counsel for Advocacy of the Small Business Administration for comment, if any.

c) Each agency shall endeavor to provide notice of each regulatory flexibility agenda to small entities or their representatives through direct notification or publication of the agenda in publications likely to be obtained by such small entities and shall invite comments upon each subject area on the agenda.

d) Nothing in this section precludes an agency from considering or acting on any matter not included in a regulatory flexibility agenda, or requires an agency to consider or act on any matter listed in such agenda.

(Added Pub. L. 96-354, Sec. 3(a), Sept. 19, 1980, 94 Stat. 1166.)

SEC. 603. Initial Regulatory Flexibility Analysis [Cite: 5 USC 603]

a) Whenever an agency is required by section 553 of this title, or any other law, to publish general notice of proposed rulemaking for any proposed rule, or publishes a notice of proposed rulemaking for an interpretative rule involving the internal revenue laws of the United States, the agency shall prepare and make available for public comment an initial regulatory flexibility analysis. Such analysis shall describe the impact of the proposed rule on small entities. The initial regulatory flexibility analysis or a summary shall be published in the *Federal Register* at the time of the publication of general notice of proposed rulemaking for the rule. The agency shall transmit a copy of the initial regulatory flexibility analysis to the Chief Counsel for Advocacy of the Small Business Administration. In the case of an interpretative rule involving the internal revenue laws of the United States, this chapter applies to interpretative rules published in the *Federal Register* for codification in the Code of Federal Regulations, but only to the extent that such interpretative rules impose on small entities a collection of information requirement.

b) Each initial regulatory flexibility analysis required under this section shall contain—

(1) a description of the reasons why action by the agency is being considered;

(2) a succinct statement of the objectives of, and legal basis for, the proposed rule;

(3) a description of and, where feasible, an estimate of the number of small entities to which the proposed rule will apply;

(4) a description of the projected reporting, recordkeeping and other compliance requirements of the proposed rule, including an estimate of the classes of small entities which will be subject to the requirement and the type of professional skills necessary for preparation of the report or record;

(5) an identification, to the extent practicable, of all relevant Federal rules which may duplicate, overlap or conflict with the proposed rule.

c) Each initial regulatory flexibility analysis shall also contain a description of any significant alternatives to the proposed rule which accomplish the stated objectives of applicable statutes and which minimize any significant economic impact of the proposed rule on small entities. Consistent with the stated objectives of applicable statutes, the analysis shall discuss significant alternatives such as—

(1) the establishment of differing compliance or reporting requirements or timetables that take into account the resources available to small entities;

(2) the clarification, consolidation, or simplification of compliance and reporting requirements under the rule for such small entities;

(3) the use of performance rather than design standards; and

(4) an exemption from coverage of the rule, or any part thereof, for such small entities.

(Added Pub. L. 96-354, Sec. 3(a), Sept. 19, 1980, 94 Stat. 1166; amended Pub. L. 104-121, title II, Sec. 241(a)(1), Mar. 29, 1996, 110 Stat. 864.)

SEC. 604. Final Regulatory Flexibility Analysis [Cite: 5 USC 604]

a) When an agency promulgates a final rule under section 553 of this title, after being required by that section or any other law to publish a general notice of proposed rulemaking, or promulgates a final interpretative rule involving the internal revenue laws of the United States as described in section 603(a), the agency shall prepare a final regulatory flexibility analysis. Each final regulatory flexibility analysis shall contain—

(1) a succinct statement of the need for, and objectives of, the rule;

(2) a summary of the significant issues raised by the public comments in response to the initial regulatory flexibility analysis, a summary of the assessment of the agency of such issues, and a statement of any changes made in the proposed rule as a result of such comments;

(3) a description of and an estimate of the number of small entities to which the rule will apply or an explanation of why no such estimate is available;

(4) a description of the projected reporting, recordkeeping and other compliance requirements of the rule, including an estimate of the classes of small entities which will be subject to the requirement and the type of professional skills necessary for preparation of the report or record; and

(5) a description of the steps the agency has taken to minimize the significant economic impact on small entities consistent with the stated objectives of applicable statutes, including a statement of the factual, policy, and legal reasons for selecting the alternative adopted in the final rule and why each one of the other significant

alternatives to the rule considered by the agency which affect the impact on small entities was rejected.

b) The agency shall make copies of the final regulatory flexibility analysis available to members of the public and shall publish in the Federal Register such analysis or a summary thereof.

(Added Pub. L. 96-354, Sec. 3(a), Sept. 19, 1980, 94 Stat. 1167; amended Pub. L. 104-121, title II, Sec. 241(b), Mar. 29, 1996, 110 Stat. 864.)

SEC. 605. Avoidance of Duplicative or Unnecessary Analyses [Cite: 5 USC 605]

a) Any Federal agency may perform the analyses required by sections 602, 603, and 604 of this title in conjunction with or as a part of any other agenda or analysis required by any other law if such other analysis satisfies the provisions of such sections.

b) Sections 603 and 604 of this title shall not apply to any proposed or final rule if the head of the agency certifies that the rule will not, if promulgated, have a significant economic impact on a substantial number of small entities. If the head of the agency makes a certification under the preceding sentence, the agency shall publish such certification in the *Federal Register* at the time of publication of general notice of proposed rulemaking for the rule or at the time of publication of the final rule, along with a statement providing the factual basis for such certification. The agency shall provide such certification and statement to the Chief Counsel for Advocacy of the Small Business Administration.

c) In order to avoid duplicative action, an agency may consider a series of closely related rules as one rule for the purposes of sections 602, 603, 604 and 610 of this title.

(Added Pub. L. 96-354, Sec. 3(a), Sept. 19, 1980, 94 Stat. 1167; amended Pub. L. 104-121, title II, Sec. 243(a), Mar. 29, 1996, 110 Stat. 866.)

SEC. 606. Effect on Other Law [Cite: 5 USC 606]

The requirements of sections 603 and 604 of this title do not alter in any manner standards otherwise applicable by law to agency action.

(Added Pub. L. 96-354, Sec. 3(a), Sept. 19, 1980, 94 Stat. 1168.)

SEC. 607. Preparation of analyses [cite: 5 usc 607]

In complying with the provisions of sections 603 and 604 of this title, an agency may provide either a quantifiable or numerical description of the effects of a proposed rule or alternatives to the proposed rule, or more general descriptive statements if quantification is not practicable or reliable.

(Added Pub. L. 96-354, Sec. 3(a), Sept. 19, 1980, 94 Stat. 1168.)

SEC. 608. Procedure for Waiver or Delay of Completion [Cite: 5 USC 608]

a) An agency head may waive or delay the completion of some or all of the requirements of section 603 of this title by publishing in the Federal Register, not later than the date of publication of the final rule, a written finding, with reasons therefore, that the final rule is being promulgated in response to an emergency that makes compliance or timely compliance with the provisions of section 603 of this title impracticable.

b) Except as provided in section 605(b), an agency head may not waive the requirements of section 604 of this title. An agency head may delay the completion of the requirements of section 604 of this title for a period of not more than one hundred and eighty days after the date of publication in the Federal Register of a final rule by publishing in the Federal Register, not later than such date of publication, a written finding, with reasons therefore, that the final rule is being promulgated in response to an emergency that makes timely compliance with the provisions of section 604 of this title impracticable. If the agency has not prepared a final regulatory analysis pursuant to section 604 of this title within one hundred and eighty days from the date of publication of the final rule, such rule shall lapse and have no effect. Such rule shall not be repromulgated until a final regulatory flexibility analysis has been completed by the agency.

(Added Pub. L. 96-354, Sec. 3(a), Sept. 19, 1980, 94 Stat. 1168.)

SEC. 609. Procedures for Gathering Comments [Cite: 5 USC 609]

(a) When any rule is promulgated which will have a significant economic impact on a substantial number of small entities, the head of the agency promulgating the rule or the official of the agency with statutory responsibility for the promulgation of the rule shall assure that small entities have been given an opportunity to participate in the rulemaking for the rule through the reasonable use of techniques such as—

   (1) the inclusion in an advanced notice of proposed rulemaking, if issued, of a statement that the proposed rule may have a significant economic effect on a substantial number of small entities;

   (2) the publication of general notice of proposed rulemaking in publications likely to be obtained by small entities;

   (3) the direct notification of interested small entities;

   (4) the conduct of open conferences or public hearings concerning the rule for small entities including soliciting and receiving comments over computer networks; and

   (5) the adoption or modification of agency procedural rules to reduce the cost or complexity of participation in the rulemaking by small entities.

(b) Prior to publication of an initial regulatory flexibility analysis which a covered agency is required to conduct by this chapter—

   (1) a covered agency shall notify the Chief Counsel for Advocacy of the Small Business Administration and provide the Chief Counsel with information on the potential impacts of the proposed rule on small entities and the type of small entities that might be affected;

   (2) not later than 15 days after the date of receipt of the materials described in paragraph (1), the Chief Counsel shall identify individuals representative of affected small entities for the purpose

of obtaining advice and recommendations from those individuals about the potential impacts of the proposed rule;

(3) the agency shall convene a review panel for such rule consisting wholly of full time Federal employees of the office within the agency responsible for carrying out the proposed rule, the Office of Information and Regulatory Affairs within the Office of Management and Budget, and the Chief Counsel;

(4) the panel shall review any material the agency has prepared in connection with this chapter, including any draft proposed rule, collect advice and recommendations of each individual small entity representative identified by the agency after consultation with the Chief Counsel, on issues related to subsections 603(b), paragraphs (3), (4) and

(5) and 603(c); (5) not later than 60 days after the date a covered agency convenes a review panel pursuant to paragraph (3), the review panel shall report on the comments of the small entity representatives and its findings as to issues related to subsections 603(b), paragraphs (3), (4) and (5) and 603(c), provided that such report shall be made public as part of the rulemaking record; and

(6) where appropriate, the agency shall modify the proposed rule, the initial regulatory flexibility analysis or the decision on whether an initial regulatory flexibility analysis is required.

(c) An agency may in its discretion apply subsection (b) to rules that the agency intends to certify under subsection 605(b), but the agency believes may have a greater than *de minimis* impact on a substantial number of small entities.

(d) For purposes of this section, the term "covered agency" means the Environmental Protection Agency and the Occupational Safety and Health Administration of the Department of Labor.

(e) The Chief Counsel for Advocacy, in consultation with the individuals identified in subsection (b)(2), and with the Administrator of the Office of Information and Regulatory Affairs within the Office of Management and Budget, may waive the requirements of subsections (b)(3), (b)(4), and (b)(5) by including in the rulemaking record a written finding, with reasons therefore, that those requirements would not advance the effective participation of small entities in the rulemaking process. For purposes of this subsection, the factors to be considered in making such a finding are as follows:

(1) In developing a proposed rule, the extent to which the covered agency consulted with individuals representative of affected small entities with respect to the potential impacts of the rule and took such concerns into consideration.

(2) Special circumstances requiring prompt issuance of the rule.

(3) Whether the requirements of subsection (b) would provide the individuals identified in subsection (b)(2) with a competitive advantage relative to other small entities.

(Added Pub. L. 96-354, Sec. 3(a), Sept. 19, 1980, 94 Stat. 1168; amended Pub. L. 104-121, title II, Sec. 244(a), Mar. 29, 1996, 110 Stat. 867.)

SEC. 610. Periodic Review of Rules [Cite: 5 USC 610]

(a) Within one hundred and eighty days after the effective date of this chapter, each agency shall publish in the *Federal Register* a plan for the periodic review of the rules issued by the agency which have or will have a significant economic impact upon a substantial number of small entities. Such plan may be amended by the agency at any time by publishing the revision in the *Federal Register*. The purpose of the review shall be to determine whether such rules should be continued without change, or should be amended or rescinded, consistent with the stated objectives of applicable statutes, to minimize any significant economic impact of the rules upon a substantial number of such small entities. The plan shall provide for the review of all such agency rules existing on the effective date of this chapter within ten years of that date and for the review of such rules adopted after the effective date of this chapter within ten years of the publication of such rules as the final rule. If the head of the agency determines that completion of the review of existing rules is not feasible by the established date, he shall so certify in a statement published in the *Federal Register* and may extend the completion date by one year at a time for a total of not more than five years.

(b) In reviewing rules to minimize any significant economic impact of the rule on a substantial number of small entities in a manner consistent with the stated objectives of applicable statutes, the agency shall consider the following factors—

(1) the continued need for the rule;

    (2) the nature of complaints or comments received concerning the rule from the public;

    (3) the complexity of the rule;

    (4) the extent to which the rule overlaps, duplicates or conflicts with other Federal rules, and, to the extent feasible, with State and local governmental rules; and

    (5) the length of time since the rule has been evaluated or the degree to which technology, economic conditions, or other factors have changed in the area affected by the rule.

(c) Each year, each agency shall publish in the Federal Register a list of the rules which have a significant economic impact on a substantial number of small entities, which are to be reviewed pursuant to this section during the succeeding twelve months. The list shall include a brief description of each rule and the need for and legal basis of such rule and shall invite public comment upon the rule.

(Added Pub. L. 96-354, Sec. 3(a), Sept. 19, 1980, 94 Stat. 1169.)

SEC. 611. Judicial Review [Cite: 5 USC 611]

(a) -

    (1) For any rule subject to this chapter, a small entity that is adversely affected or aggrieved by final agency action is entitled to judicial review of agency compliance with the requirements of sections 601, 604, 605(b), 608(b), and 610 in accordance with chapter 7. Agency compliance with sections 607 and 609(a) shall be judicially reviewable in connection with judicial review of section 604.

    (2) Each court having jurisdiction to review such rule for compliance with section 553, or under any other provision of law, shall have jurisdiction to review any claims of noncompliance with sections 601, 604, 605(b), 608(b), and 610 in accordance with chapter 7. Agency compliance with sections 607 and 609(a) shall be judicially reviewable in connection with judicial review of section 604.

    (3) (A) A small entity may seek such review during the period beginning on the date of final agency action and ending one year later, except that where a provision of law requires that an action

challenging a final agency action be commenced before the expiration of one year, such lesser period shall apply to an action for judicial review under this section.

(B) In the case where an agency delays the issuance of a final regulatory flexibility analysis pursuant to section 608(b) of this chapter, an action for judicial review under this section shall be filed not later than—

  i.   one year after the date the analysis is made available to the public, or

  ii.   where a provision of law requires that an action challenging a final agency regulation be commenced before the expiration of the 1-year period, the number of days specified in such provision of law that is after the date the analysis is made available to the public.

(4) In granting any relief in an action under this section, the court shall order the agency to take corrective action consistent with this chapter and chapter 7, including, but not limited to—

  A. remanding the rule to the agency, and

  B. deferring the enforcement of the rule against small entities unless the court finds that continued enforcement of the rule is in the public interest.

(5) Nothing in this subsection shall be construed to limit the authority of any court to stay the effective date of any rule or provision thereof under any other provision of law or to grant any other relief in addition to the requirements of this section.

(b) In an action for the judicial review of a rule, the regulatory flexibility analysis for such rule, including an analysis prepared or corrected pursuant to paragraph (a)(4), shall constitute part of the entire record of agency action in connection with such review.

(c) Compliance or noncompliance by an agency with the provisions of this chapter shall be subject to judicial review only in accordance with this section.

(d) Nothing in this section bars judicial review of any other impact statement or similar analysis required by any other law if judicial review of such statement or analysis is otherwise permitted by law.

(Added Pub. L. 96-354, Sec. 3(a), Sept. 19, 1980, 94 Stat. 1169; amended Pub. L. 104-121, title II, Sec. 242, Mar. 29, 1996, 110 Stat. 865.)

SEC. 612. Reports and Intervention Rights [Cite: 5 USC 612]

(a) The Chief Counsel for Advocacy of the Small Business Administration shall monitor agency compliance with this chapter and shall report at least annually thereon to the President and to the Committees on the Judiciary and Small Business of the Senate and House of Representatives.

(b) The Chief Counsel for Advocacy of the Small Business Administration is authorized to appear as *amicus curiae* in any action brought in a court of the United States to review a rule. In any such action, the Chief Counsel is authorized to present his or her views with respect to compliance with this chapter, the adequacy of the rulemaking record with respect to small entities and the effect of the rule on small entities.

(c) A court of the United States shall grant the application of the Chief Counsel for Advocacy of the Small Business Administration to appear in any such action for the purposes described in subsection (b).

(Added Pub. L. 96-354, Sec. 3(a), Sept. 19, 1980, 94 Stat. 1170; amended Pub. L. 104-121, title II, Sec. 243(b), Mar. 29, 1996, 110 Stat. 866.)

The following is an excerpt from the Dodd-Frank Wall Street Reform and Consumer Protection Act of 2010 (P.L. 11-203), amending the Small Business Regulatory Enforcement Fairness Act of 1996 (P.L. 104-121).

Sec. 1100G. Small Business Fairness and Regulatory Transparency

(a) PANEL REQUIREMENT.—Section 609(d) of title 5, United States Code, is amended by striking "means the" and all that follows and inserting the following: "means—

"(1) the Environmental Protection Agency;

"(2) the Consumer Financial Protection Bureau of the Federal Reserve System; and

"(3) the Occupational Safety and Health Administration of the Department of Labor.".

(b) INITIAL REGULATORY FLEXIBILITY ANALYSIS.—Section 603 of title 5, United States Code, is amended by adding at the end the following:

"(d)(1) For a covered agency, as defined in section 609(d)(2), each initial regulatory flexibility analysis shall include a description of—

"(A)   any projected increase in the cost of credit for small entities;

"(B)   any significant alternatives to the proposed rule which accomplish the stated objectives of applicable statutes and which minimize any increase in the cost of credit for small entities; and

"(C)   advice and recommendations of representatives of small entities relating to issues described in subparagraphs (A) and (B) and subsection (b).

H. R. 4173—738

"(2) A covered agency, as defined in section 609(d)(2), shall, for purposes of complying with paragraph (1)(C)—

"(A)   identify representatives of small entities in consultation with the Chief Counsel for Advocacy of the Small Business Administration; and

"(B)   collect advice and recommendations from the representatives identified under subparagraph (A) relating to issues described in subparagraphs (A) and (B) of paragraph (1) and subsection (b).".

(c) FINAL REGULATORY FLEXIBILITY ANALYSIS.—Section 604(a) of title 5, United States Code, is amended—

(1) in paragraph (4), by striking "and" at the end;

(2) in paragraph (5), by striking the period at the end and inserting "; and"; and

by adding at the end the following:

"(6) for a covered agency, as defined in section 609(d)(2), a description of the steps the agency has taken to minimize any additional cost of credit for small entities.".

SEC. 1100H. Effective Date

Except as otherwise provided in this subtitle and the amendments made by this subtitle, this subtitle and the amendments made by this subtitle, other than sections 1081 and 1082, shall become effective on the designated transfer date.

End Notes

[1] Regulatory Flexibility Act, Pub. L. No. 96-354, 94 Stat. 1164 (codified at 5 U.S.C. § 601).

[2] 15 U.S.C. § 632. The North American Industry Classification System (NAICS) breaks down industry sectors and is used to identify the industry, governmental and nonprofit sectors an agency intends to regulate. Size standard regulations specifying size standards and governing their use are set forth in Title 13, Code of Federal Regulations, 13 CFR §121.

[3] Small Business Regulatory Enforcement Fairness Act of 1996, Pub. L. No. 104-121, 110 Stat. 857 (codified at 5 U.S.C. § 601 et seq.).

[4] 5 U.S.C § 553(b).

[5] Id .at § 553(a).

[6] Id. at § 553(b)(A).

[7] 5 U.S.C. § 601(2).

[8] 5 U.S.C. § 605(b).

[9] See North Carolina Fisheries Ass'n v. Daley, 27 F. Supp. 2d 650 (E.D. Va. 1998).

[10] 5 U.S.C. § 603(a).

[11] Id.

[12] Exec. Order No. 13,272, § 3(b).

[13] 5 U.S.C. § 603(b)-(c).

[14] Bowen v. AHA, 476 U.S. 610, 643 (186); National Ass'n of Home Health Agencies v. Schweiker, 690 F.2d 932, 949 (D.C. Cir. 1982); Chocolate Mfrs. Ass'n v. Block, 755 F.2d 1098, 1103 (4th Cir. 1985).

[15] Source: Title 5, Part I, Chapter 6 from U.S. Code Online via GPO Access [wais.access.gpo.gov]

INDEX

monetary policy, 6, 71

N

natural gas, 7, 11, 60, 61, 62, 63, 134
natural gas pipeline, 60, 61, 134
network elements, 39, 41, 52, 122, 127, 130
New York Stock Exchange, 142
North America, 62, 134, 173
NPR, 93, 118
Nuclear Regulatory Commission (NRC), 7,
    11, 17, 94, 95, 96, 109, 111, 112, 115,
    141, 142

O

Occupational Safety and Health Act
    (OSHA), 8, 96, 147, 156
Office of Management and Budget (OMB),
    vii, 1, 3, 5, 167
officials, 140
oil, 7, 11, 60, 61, 83, 132
operations, 31, 36, 45, 72, 98, 100, 118,
    127, 128
opportunities, 15, 121, 129, 130
organ, 35
organize, 93
outreach, 38, 127, 154, 156
overlap, 48, 152, 162
oversight, vii, 1, 14, 22, 56, 58, 66, 71, 91,
    97, 98
ownership structure, 33
ownership, 33, 49, 55

P

participants, 6, 7, 19, 20, 23, 41, 98
penalties, 26, 61, 70, 73, 96
permit, 108, 129, 144
persons with disabilities, 128
petroleum, 132
pipeline, 61, 132
plants, 134
platform, 129

playing, 62, 129, 146, 157
policy, ix, 4, 24, 32, 59, 71, 80, 83, 107,
    110, 113, 118, 145, 148, 150, 156, 163
policy makers, 83
pools, 132
population, 24, 63, 74, 86, 102, 104, 121,
    138, 142, 146, 160
potential benefits, 154
power lines, 122
power plants, 94, 95
PRC, 8, 97, 109, 110, 142
preferential treatment, 146, 156
preparation, 4, 78, 110, 150, 151, 152, 156,
    162, 163
preservation, 20, 22
president, 3, 60, 171
President Clinton, 3
President Obama, 3
presidential authority, vii, 1, 3
prevention, 25
price changes, 43
principles, 35, 56, 66
private investment, 120
private sector, 9, 93
private sector employers, 93
probe, 39
procedural rule, 134, 166
professionals, 30
profit, 141, 142, 159
programming, 36
project, 78, 134
proposed regulations, 146
proposition, 86
protection, 16, 56, 62, 82, 83, 94, 100, 104
Public Company Accounting Oversight
    Board, 143
public concern, 23
public financing, 60
public health, 7, 94
public interest, 22, 24, 148, 170
public policy, 146, 150, 157
public safety, 34, 120, 127
publishing, 122, 165, 168

T

U

V